CW01501960

– and that I did occasionally play c
and not very well –

so I thought it might at least be worth jotting all those things down....

What I realised as I was making these notes about my marginal involvement in cricket was that it fits very much in with the pattern of the rest of my life where there is a distinct North / South Divide – which is where the title of this series of rambling utterances is derived from.

While I was living in the South – well, "south-ish" anyway – of the country, although I played cricket occasionally, I never actually went to watch a game anywhere.

Conversely, since I have been living in the North of the country, I have watched a lot of cricket but never played any... Spooky, eh...?

Cricket And the Younger Me...

I didn't really appreciate cricket when I was younger. It's not really the sort of game that you can play 1 or 2 a side in the garden or the park as easily as you can football because one poor soul always ends up getting run ragged trying to find the ball that has been whacked for miles.

Plus we only had - for the most part - 5-day test cricket on the TV at the time – none of the exciting short format games that have been introduced in recent years - so it was very much an acquired taste.

We did have cricket at school – but it was only for a few weeks during the summer term and I don't really remember ever being taught how to do anything properly and we certainly never had enough time in the sports lesson to have any proper sort of game.

NORTH / SOUTH DIVIDE

Volume 3: Cricket & Baseball

By Paul Breeze

Interesting Books...
...Fascinating Subjects!

POSH UP NORTH
Publishing

www.poshupnorth.com

Publishing History

Bobcats Review was originally published in 1995 by Posh Up North Publishing

This edition published in Great Britain in October 2021 by
Ice Hockey Review, which is an imprint of
Posh Up North Publishing, Beckenham Road, Wallasey, United Kingdom

ISBN-13: 978-1-909643-46-8

LIST OF CONTENTS

Cover Photos

Front Cover:
A view of the Pakistan v Australia game in the Cricket World Cup, 1999 (Photo by Paul Breeze)
University of Central Lancashire baseball team, May 1997 (Photo by Jill Peacock)
Paul playing for Preston Bobcats at a tournament in Warrington, May 1994 (Photo by Hanja Ihnen)
Paul umpiring a baseball game at Budisov in the Czech Republic, 1996
Back Cover: Paul ready battle in the Germans v Czechs game in the Czech Republic, 1996

Between the showers – lunch break at Old Trafford. You can just see the West Indies players on the pitch in the background (Photo by Posh Up North Publishing)

PART ONE: CRICKET

This book comes about as a direct result of my reading - and very much enjoying - a book by my friend Stuart Latham about his lifelong love of - and involvement with – the game of cricket.

I was very much impressed by Stuart's family background in the sport and was fascinated to read about the places he has been and the people he has met - and I thought to myself:

"Huh! If I wrote a book about MY connection with cricket, it would only stretch to about three pages...!"

But it did set me thinking.

And it reminded me that Lucy and I had worked as media volunteers at the Cricket World Cup in 1999

– and that we had been members of Blackpool Cricket Club for 10 years when we lived there

4

We played French Cricket when I used to go to Cubs and that was a bit more fun as there were lots of people playing and the ball never went very far as we played indoors in the sports hall of the local school where the pack meetings took place.

For the uninitiated, that is a game where the batsman would hold the bat in front of his shins, which acted as the wicket. Everybody else would stand round in a circle and, when the ball came to them, they'd try and bowl it to hit his legs to get him out and the batsmen would pivot round to hit the ball away with the bat.

We also used to play British Bulldog at Cubs. Do people actually play that any more? Too rough? Too jingoistic…? Offensive to animals…? Who knows…

And there was another game that we played occasionally, which everybody seemed to enjoy and which I have never come across anywhere else. It is worth mentioning here – if only for the benefit of future social historians - as I am sure it is probably banned these days.
We would all stand around in a big circle, facing inwards with our eyes closed. We would hold our hands behind our back, palms open, and the scout leader would quietly place a rolled up newspaper in somebody's hand.

The recipient of the newspaper was then supposed to batter the person on their immediate right in the circle on the back and shoulders with the paper and he, in turn, had to run around the outside of the circle to get away from the onslaught.

Once the runner had completed the circuit and got back to his place, the battering would cease, everybody would close their eyes again and the batterer (for want of a better word) would noiselessly walk around the circle and place the newspaper in somebody else's hands…

And this normally went on until the newspaper had fallen into shreds and we moved on to some other jolly 1970s character building activity.

Cricket At School
(But Not Very Much Of It...)

Not being especially good at sports, I never really enjoyed our sports lessons at school very much.

I didn't mind having a kick-about at football with a few friends so long as nobody expected me to do anything spectacular (or go in goal – yuk! too muddy...) but at school there were always lots of people who were really good at these things, played for local teams or whatever, had all the gear and generally gave you the feeling of being a waste of space.

I remember once during a break time playground game asking the "captain" of the team that I had been put with where he wanted to play and he replied somewhat disparagingly while walking away from me, shaking his head... "f**cking defence...."

At our school – by which I mean senior / comprehensive school (age 11 plus...) here – not junior school / primary school, where we used to play games in our normal class groups which was more fun based – we had a double lesson of "games" once a week and a single lesson of PE or swimming.

For the swimming / PE lessons we were in class groups and it was split between boys and girls. During the autumn and spring terms, the boys used the pool for half of the time and the girls were in the gym - and vice–versa.

During the summer term we did athletics outside on the school field in those sessions, weather permitting.

I seem to think that we had two classes combined for the PE and swimming lessons to make up the right numbers. In our case, in the first year for example – aged 11 - I was in class 1F, which was the top class.

Don't ask me why it was called 1F as I have no idea. The next class down but with broadly similarly clever people was 1Y – and I don't know why it was called 1Y either – and it had people like Wiggy, Richard Ellis, Darren Jinks and Alan Platt in it so we all got on well together. So, the combined boys of 1F and 1Y did swimming together while the combined girls of 1F and 1Y did PE and vice-versa.

The rest of the classes in the first year – and I don't remember now what they all were but they different letters like 1K, 1H etc continuing down to 1W, which was bottom for some reason.

The top class in the second year was called 2H – which I was also in – and that didn't really make sense either....

Although I wasn't a very strong swimmer – and was not very gymnastic either – I didn't mind those sessions so much because they were held in smaller groups and I knew most of the other people quite well.

The "games lessons" were different as it was the whole year group thrown in together.

This might be rambling off the point slightly, but a bit of background information would help the reader to understand this previous statement.

Based on where I lived when I was little, there were two primary schools in Stanground that I might have gone to. One was St John's School on Chapel Street down on the way to the Church in "Old Stanground" and the other was Southfields which was a newer school up in the other direction at the top of the Lawson Estate, as much of the hitherto new build area used to be known, at least when it was being built – but not necessarily in my day.

As far, as I can tell they were both more or less equi-distant from my house and I did, in later years, attend activities at both – school and pathfinders at Southfields, Cubs and summer play schemes at St John's - so I did get to know kids from both areas over the years – but I really don't know how I came to go to Southfields rather than St John's.

I asked my mum about this, and she said that there had never been any sort of discussion or decision to be made about which school I should go to - and everybody from along where we used to live just automatically went to Southfields. So there we have it.

I daresay there must have been some administrative demarcation line that determined who went to which school but I don't know where it might have been. I do know that everybody who lived on

Chapel Street went to St John's School but am not sure about people living at the top end of Coneygree Road up near the Carpenters Arms as I never knew any kids who lived along there.

Anyway, as a rough guide - for the most part, children from the Old Stanground / Chapel Street area went to St John's School and kids from the area to the south of Coneygree Road and stretching along to Ellwood Avenue, Southfields Avenue and so on went to Southfields School.

Just leaping ahead slightly here – but it is interesting, if not entirely relevant to me playing cricket - when we went to "big school" at age 11, the majority of us from Southfields went up to Stanground Comprehensive School, in whose catchment area we all lived.

One person that I know of went to Kings School in town – which is connected to the Cathedral and had very strict entrance criteria - and it was also possible for practicing Roman Catholics to go to the catholic St John Fisher School in town.

It was also possible for people from our area to go to Orton Longueville School instead – they apparently had better reputation for maths or something. You had to get a bus to go there and we would often see the kids waiting for the Orton bus sitting in the doorway of the Co-Op on the Parade as we were walking up to Southfields.

They always had a smarter uniform than we did with a dark blazer, blue shirts and a tie but always looked really miserable hunched there in all weathers waiting for the bus!

Anyway, back to Southfields and Stanground.... The B1092 road was a very important landmark for us when I was little. It is actually called Whittlesey Road and we often just used to refer to it at the time as the "Main Road".

On the other side of the main road was the Oakdale estate based along the length of Oakdale Avenue which joined the Whittlesey Road at both of its extremities, more or less in the same way as Coneygree Road did on our side.

There was a separate primary school for children from the Oakdale estate but a lot of people from that area also went to Southfields school so I knew a lot of people from over there as well.

Starting off at age 4 at Southfields Infant School for 3 years, and then having 4 years at the neighbouring Junior school, there were a lot of children from the area who I had known and grown up with.

So, when at age 11 most of us then graduated to the Stanground Comprehensive School, it was a bit of a shock because we then found ourselves all in a much bigger year group, not only with the kids from St John's School – some of who I knew already – and the kids from Oakdale – most of whom I didn't – but there were also people from the wider area such as Fletton, Farcet and Yaxley, none of whom, it had ever occurred to me might ever have existed before then!

I'd been fairly comfortable at Southfields and gradually rose to become a biggish fish in the small primary school pond – and I was, dare I say it, on the "cleverer" side in terms of academic achievement.

However, I readily acknowledged a more reduced status alongside the better sports players – the Danny MacIntryes who were always good at football and played for the school teams and the Richard Ellises whose dads played for their works teams and taught them to swim at an early age etc,

As such, it was most galling when, at the big school, there was an influx of loads more people who were just as academically clever as me and who all had their own Danny MacIntryres and Richard Ellises who were infinitely better at all things sporting.

We were all placed in Houses when we arrived at Stanground Comp and these were based on geographical location and, therefore, which primary school you had gone to.

The houses were named after Saints (nobody seems to know why) and we had:

Peter House for people from Yaxley (house colour: yellow)
Mary House for people from Farcet (house colour: maroon)
Stephen House for People from Oakdale (house colour: red)
Thomas House for People from St Johns (house colour: white)
and James (blue) and Andrew (green) Houses for people from Southfields.

So basically there were at least three times as many people in my year group at Comprehensive school than there had been at Junior school.

I seem to recall that we had three classes per year group at Southfields – both infants and junior school, with around 30 pupils per class each time.

For the benefit of anybody who might wish to answer questions about my "Life and Times" on Mastermind at some point in the future, my class teachers at Southfields were:

Infant School: Mrs Sutton / Miss Hill (who became Mrs Brown mid-year) / Mrs Brinkler

Junior School: Mrs Hunns / Mr Sutton / Miss Burgess / Mr Walker

Anyway, assuming 50% of the class make up was girls – although, apparently, my age group were the first generation to have more boys than girls due to a lack of wars for them to get killed in – so it might not be a completely accurate split, but it would certainly explain why it always seemed more difficult to get girlfriends....

Thus, out of a theoretical 15 boys in a class group, (yes, I know girls can play football as well – but back then it just didn't happen, however good they might have been and however wrong we might all feel it was...) if you were, say, ranked 13th or 14th in terms of football ability – behind the fat kid who very good in goal but ahead of the wimpy kid who always had serious health issues – but were in a group that you had more or less grown with, you could cope with being only ever being substitute and occasionally included if a few other people were missing.

But in terms of a whole year group (ie school team) with 3 classes and 45 theoretical boys, there would be 30 or 40 boys ahead of you in the pecking order so you wouldn't get much of a chance.

(I was actually quite a fast runner in those days and represented my school at the City sports on a couple of occasions - but we'll cover that some other time...)

So, if you then multiply that year group into Comprehensive school proportions of around 120 other theoretical boys who are all better than you at football, rugby etc, you will then appreciate my earlier comment about why I didn't very much enjoy our weekly "games" lessons.

Those 120 or so boys were split into a morning games group and an afternoon games group – and then they were further split into three separate activities which we did over the autumn and winter months – football, rugby and hockey.

I was always lucky enough to be in an afternoon games group which meant that we had our sports sessions just before home time so I didn't have to spend the rest of the day carrying smelly gear and damp towels around in my bag.

Joanne Harrison has kindly reminded me that the girls played hockey and netball during the winter terms and rounders and tennis during the summer. I think - with the benefit of hindsight – I would have probably preferred to play rounders with them, to be honest...

She tells me they also did a term of lacrosse one year – with some equipment borrowed from somewhere or other.

If you are not familiar with lacrosse, Lucy tells me that it is rather like ice hockey only played on grass without the safety gear - where the players wield aggressive looking sticks in the air, and I can only assume that it didn't catch on as nobody else has ever mentioned this.

So - we did nominally learn cricket at school. But we only did cricket during the summer term – ie after the Easter holidays - and only half of us did that while the other half did tennis – and all that was weather permitting.

I was never actually in the tennis games class at school and never learnt to play it properly, ever. I did used to play on the school courts a lot during lunchtimes and evenings with school friends and later in Peterborough Central Park on the grass courts and at various leisure centres - but only ever in a very amateurish way.

Now, if you take my own experience as the typical exposure to learning cricket that a young male of my age and background had in the late 1970s and early 1980s, you can understand how it has lost popularity as a game over the past decades.

While I can quite clearly remember hours and hours of standing on a waterlogged school field freezing cold and shivering through games lesson after games lesson of football and rugby – and, to a lesser extent, hockey with its endless pointless stoppages for silly infringements (feet...! etc) - I have hardly any recollection at all of any meaningful time having been spent learning the skills or playing cricket as a school activity.

I do recall us being out on the field with the bag of cricket equipment – and being told about the importance of the protective "box" - and noticing that the batting gloves had spikes on them...

I know that we wore our gym (indoor) gear for cricket – ie white t-shirts and white shorts, which made it uncomfortable when you buckled the pads around your legs – but as for any sort of batting or bowling practice or any sort of actual game – my mind is a complete blank.

I do know that the school had a cricket team and probably an after-school cricket "club" of some sort so can only assume that anybody who had any real interest went along to that.

I presume that it was pretty much the same in drama and music and "practical" things like woodwork and metalwork, where they made a token gesture of teaching a few basics just to fulfil the requirement and anybody who had a particular aptitude was probably given further encouragement outside of normal class time.

Anyway, and the one and only time that I ever played in a proper cricket match in the whole of my life – with the full complement of players on each side – I did actually rather enjoy it.

It was the annual Staff v Sixth Form match at my school at the end of the school year and I was on the sixth form team – probably to make up the numbers.

We also had a staff v sixth form football match around that time, which I also played in – don't ask me how / why because I have never been any good at football either.

I clearly remember that the football match was quite an evenly matched affair although we eventually lost 4-2 to the staff - but I haven't the dimmest clue what the score or the result of the cricket match was.

In fact the only thing that I do remember about the cricket match was that, late on in the game, I volunteered to have a bowl – and, with my very first ball, I bowled out our headmaster!

I'd never bowled a cricket ball properly in my life before and based my technique on what I'd seen one of my friends' dads doing years before when we having a knock out on the playing field where he had basically stood rooted at the bowler's end and just sent casual overarms over towards the stumps to give everybody some batting practice.

In all fairness - and with a lot of hindsight - I do think that Mr Barker (our headmaster – famous for being the first comprehensively educated individual to become a senior school headmaster anywhere…) was probably expecting me to take some sort of run up before dispatching the ball and the ball itself - when it did arrive - was such a terrible one that he was probably so caught out by it that he didn't quite know what to do with it.

I seem to think he sort of clipped it and it flew off into the air for an easy catch. I'm afraid that I don't remember what happened in the rest of the over but I like to think that a total career average of 1 wicket from 1 over bowled is quite a good achievement.

Here is a photo of one of Stuart Latham's relatives – John Thomas Hearne of Middlesex and England (1867-1944) – see my review of Stuart's book for an explanation....

I reckon this would be an almost exact depiction of my headmaster's view of me when I bowled him out in the 1985 Staff v Sixth Form cricket match!

(Photo by Foster of Preston Street, Brighton)

Stanground School – James House 5th Year, 1983

Back Row: Steven Porter, Andrew Chapman, David Steels, PB, Stuart Bird, Michael Haynes, Michael Martin. Third Row: John Steels, Karl Lillicrap, Robert Flack, Steven Corr, Paul Jinks, Paul Winskill, Nathan Howell. Second Row: Janet Miller, Shuna Holman, Danny MacIntyre, Richard Stocks, Alison Gausden, Steven Anker, Graham Hill, Vicky Lack, Linda Green. Front Row: Linda Sayer, Carol Sharp, Suzanna Mankiewski, Helena Perkins, Sarah Cooke, Jackie Ashpool, Donna Clark, Anna Ginatassio, Angela Crouch.

This is, sadly, the only formal "school photo" that I ever appeared in. For some reason, in all the time I attended school from 1972 to 1985 we never had any formal class photos taken - which is sad from a "memories" point of view.

I don't see how it would have been that difficult to organise because we did have a photographer come into school every year and take individual portraits – or sibling groups if people requested them – that parents could buy prints of, so everybody from a given class will have been present queuing up for those photos to be taken anyway.

I don't know whether this was a widespread thing in the 70s and if all the other schools still took class photos or year photos on a regular basis - or if it was just at our school that they didn't - but I am wondering whether it was some sort of rebellion against the whole traditional "grammar school" scene which was quite trendy during those days – but who knows. You'd have to ask whoever it was that made the decisions.

Anyway, in 1983, somebody obviously decided to start taking group photos at our school and this is the result.

These are "house year group" photos and there are loads of these scattered around on Facebook now as they became a regular thing over the years. I am especially grateful to Sarah Cooke for posting this one in our school memories group as I had mislaid my copy.

There is quite an odd collection of people in this photo, to be honest, and most of us were never actually in the same class for anything at Stanground School.

These are people who were in James House – ie lived in the same rough geographical area as I did – and were in the same year group, ie started at age 11 for the 1978/79 academic year.

There are actually quite a few people missing from this photo who I could name off the top of my head but can only imagine had either left by the time this photo was taken or were missing on the day itself.

Of all the pupils in this photo, only about 6 stayed on in the Sixth Form – as that wasn't quite the be all and end all that it is these days – and I only recall ever having been in a class with 7 or 8 of these during my time at Stanground.

We did, however, all – apart from two or three who came along later – go to the same infant and junior schools and, over the years, I have known most of the people on this photo quite well - so it is a nice memory to have.

Just for the record – not that you'd be able to guess from this photo - the official school uniform at that time was:

- Maroon jumper (a cardigan or tank top was also allowed...)
- White, grey or blue shirt or blouse (although quite how you could possibly have three completely different colours as a "uniform" always mystified me ...)
- Charcoal grey trousers

When looking at this photo, I find it quite surprising how, despite having a - supposedly - official school uniform, hardly ANYBODY is actually wearing the same thing!

You won't be able to see it on here but I am probably not in fully correct uniform either, and am most likely wearing black trousers as charcoal grey used to be very difficult to get hold of back in those days.

You had to go to somewhere quite expensive like John Walton school outfitters in town or Marks & Spencer and, with the way we used to roll around on the floor and get muck and grass all over them, and makes holes in things - not to mention grow out of them, a lot of parents didn't think it was worth that expense.

So, people often wore black trousers – or light grey – or whatever was easily available. This was in the days before Asda and such places used to sell cheap school clothing like they do now.

In the early 1980s, there was a fashion for a while of wearing stay press trousers – which I actually think was spelt "Sta Prest" and was based on an expensive brand name of which most people – as with Crombie coats and Harrington jackets – actually wore the local market stall equivalent.

These trousers were part of the Mods and Ska culture at the time and all the ones I saw were a very light – almost silvery - grey colour. Apparently they had a special treatment so they didn't lose their crease, although as far as I can remember, everybody looked just as scruffy in these as they did in everything else.

People tended to wear them slightly short at the ankle over white socks and with black loafers or brogue shoes - so they did more or less fit in with the school uniform requirement of the day.

To be honest, I think - overall - the staff were probably just happy that everybody turned up and looked vaguely presentable....

PB with (l to r): Nikki Jude, David Gilding and Diana Pacocha presenting a fund raising cheque for an asthma charity outside the 6th Form block in 1985 (Peterborough Evening Telegraph Photo)

PB (middle) with Graham Hill (left) and Paul's brother Gary (right) in the pouring rain at Wembley Stadium before Peterborough United's Play Off win against Darlington in 2000. Just to clarify, this was not the occasion when Graham explained the point of cricket to me... (Photo by Lucy London)

Understanding Cricket – at Last...!

I was quite a mature (ish…) adult before I fully got to understand and appreciate the point of cricket.

A group of us were driving to a football match – a longish, slightly dull away trip to watch Peterborough United (possibly at Luton or Southend or somewhere like that) one of whom was my long term school friend from when I was very little, Graham Hill (no – not the racing driver, a different one… He actually had a cousin from Fletton who was also called "Graham Hill" and the two of them went with me to cubs at the same time, which might have been confusing for the uninitiated...).

Anyway, he - that is the "Stanground" Graham Hill - was patiently trying to explain how one team could score 600 runs in a game and the other team only 400 and the match still end up as a draw.

He made the point that you only actually needed to score 1 single run to win a cricket match so long as you bowled the opposition out for 0. And that it was the bowling out that mattered - more so than the scoring of runs.

All of a sudden, the penny dropped and years and years of misunderstanding were washed away.
I then realised why Mr Hill had always been more keen on being on the bowling side – as opposed to everybody else who enjoys batting – and why he once strangely insisted during one of our occasional teenage not-very-good 2 or 3 a-side games during the school holidays that my team "follow on" and have another bat (hurrah for us, I thought at the time…).

But we were just having a laugh and mucking about with a bat and a tennis ball, whereas HE was taking it all very seriously indeed and strategically setting out to try and WIN THE MATCH!

Another reason why I never got on very well with cricket – apart from maybe watching it on TV - was that when I was young I always suffered with terrible hayfever during the summer. It kicked in when I was about 7, for some reason, and after that I had to go around heavily dosed up on tablets for about 5 months of the year and also needed to avoid rolling around in the grass as much as possible.

In later years I discovered a very simple remedy for my hayfever – which I won't bother to tell you about because everybody I have ever told about it has not believed me and scoffed that it wouldn't work for them and they HAVE to take load of medication - as their hayfever is probably much worse than mine was.

Well, I can guarantee you that it probably wasn't as my hayfever used to be extremely debilitating and stopped me doing all sorts of things. Whereas now, I am completely liberated, can mow the lawn, take country walks – and I have not taken any sort of tablet for over 10 years, if not more.

Team Sheets

AUSTRALIA

Squad	Batting Order
1 Steve Waugh	1 Adam Gilchrist
2 Michael Bevan	2 Mark Waugh
3 Damien Fleming	3 Ricky Ponting
4 Paul Reiffel	4 Darren Lehman
5 Shane Warne	5 Steve Waugh
6 Mark Waugh	6 Michael Bevan
7 Shane Lee	7 Damien Martyn
8 Brendon Julian	8 Shane Warne
9 Tom Moody	9 Paul Reiffel
10 Darren Lehman	10 Damien Fleming
11 Glenn McGrath	11 Glenn McGrath
12 Adam Gilchrist	12 Brendon Julian
13 Adam Dale	
14 Ricky Ponting	
15 Damien Martyn	

PAKISTAN

Squad	Batting Order
1 Wasim Akram	1 Saeed Anwar
2 Moin Khan	2 Wajahatullah Wasti
3 Saleem Malik	3 Abdul Razzaq
4 Ijaz Ahmed	4 Ijaz Ahmed
5 Waqar Younis	5 Inziman-Ul-Haq
6 Saeed Anwar	6 Yousuf Youhana
7 Mushtaq Ahmed	7 Azhar Mahmood
8 Inziman-Ul-Haq	8 Moin Khan
9 Saqlain Mushtaq	9 Wasim Akram
10 Shahid Afridi	10 Saqlain Mushtaq
11 Azhar Mahmood	11 Shoaib Akhar
12 Abdul Razzaq	12 Shahid Afridi
13 Yousuf Youhana	
14 Shoaib Akhar	
15 Wajahatullah Wasti	

Umpires	Match Referee
Koertzen	Subba Row
Willey	

HEADINGLEY   23/05/99

Media hand-out for the Australia v Pakistan World Cup game at Headingley

A view of the Pakistan v Australia World Cup game from the media centre end at Headingley, 23rd May 1999. Pakistan are batting (Photo by Paul Breeze)

Cricket World Cup – May / June 1999

Having become involved in volunteering at major sporting events, I arranged for Lucy and I to help out with the media at the Cricket World Cup when it was played here in 1999 and we helped out at games at Headingley and Old Trafford.

23rd May 1999: Pakistan V Australia at Headingley

We (I) actually had terrible trouble finding Headingley in the first place when we went for the orientation day the day before our first game there as I didn't realise that the cricket ground was in the same place as the rugby ground. The Leeds Rhinos rugby stadium was easily visible from the road going past and the cricket ground wasn't so we spent ages and ages driving up and down getting more and more frustrated.

Anyway, once we finally managed to get in, we met up with a few old familiar faces from previous sports media events and everything went swimmingly. We were issued with our media accreditations and our free clothing goodies and had a nice walk in the sun around the historic cricket ground, identifying what was where.

Upon arriving in the media car park (which was actually the pitch of the adjacent rugby league ground...) at the crack of dawn the following morning, we saw Peter Willey (that's he of "the bowler's Holding the batsman's Willey fame...) who was going to be Umpire for the day's game and David Gower who was there as part of the TV commentary team. Later in the day on a walk around the ground, we also saw everybody's favourite retired umpire Dickie Bird who was surrounded by young fans wanting autographs.

The game was between Australia and Pakistan and it was gorgeously bright sunny day. Having learned a thing or two at previous sports tournaments we volunteered to "look after the photographers", which was quite a good job to have because sports photographers are a very hardy and independent bunch and don't really need any looking after, but this gave us a good reason to hang around the perimeter of the playing area and make sure everybody was "all right".

We also did regular circuits of the ground to the various positions where all the photographers had set themselves up - to hand out refreshments as required.

All of this meant that we were able to be out watching the game most of the time rather than being stuck inside the windowless media centre doing admin tasks.

As a matter of interest, our media centre for the tournament at Headingley was in the new building (as it was then) right behind the wicket and was covered with the blackout material that they use so that the batsman can see the white ball when it is bowled. As such, all of the windows were covered over and we had to rely on TV feeds to know what was going on.

Having said that, we were also right next to the corridor that led to the changing rooms so we did see all of the players as they came and went from the pitch.

A particular eye-opener for me was to see the gi-normous platters of fresh fruit that were taken into the Australian dressing room for them to consume during the lunch break – a huge departure from the traditional English cricket tea and cakes...!

Pakistan batted first and notched up 275 for 8 from their 50 overs. This set the Aussies the fairly modest target of 276 to win and with Mark Waugh hitting 41, captain Steve Waugh 49, Ricky Ponting 47 and Michael Bevan 61 – and everybody's favourite all rounder Shane Warne still to bat - it looked easily achievable.

But then, to universal surprise, the antipodean tail suddenly collapsed. The score was a healthy 247 for 6 when Warne came in to bat with 4 ½ overs still to go but the world's number 1 was dramatically run out for just 1 run off 6 balls and had to leave the field to the taunts from the excited Pakistani fans of "who ate all the pies!" - which actually sounds rather comical when shouted in an Asian accent...

Then Paul Reiffel was caught for 1 off his 4th ball faced with 2 and a bit overs left to go and things were looking dicey for the Aussies.

The atmosphere was absolutely electric around the ground by now. It had been a bright sunny day but it was now very gloomy in the ground and the floodlights were on. The big electronic scoreboard counted down the balls left to bowl and the runs required and the place seemed absolutely packed with over-excited Pakistani fans – considerably more numerous than had appeared to be in the ground over the course of the day.

They were all assembling in the walkways around the playing surface and were ready to swarm onto the pitch as soon as the game was over to celebrate this rather unexpected victory over Australia.

Into the last over and Damien Martyn was dismissed for 18, bowled by Wasim Akram , leaving just bowlers Damien Fleming and Glenn McGrath still to bat.

The ground security people by this time had set up an uneasy cordon around the outfield ready to leap into action with a big rope to keep the encroaching fans off the wicket at the end of the game and – to a certain extent - away from the players on the field.

At this point, my hitherto "cushy" looking job for the day of looking after the photographers took on a more sinister edge as it became clear that the gaggle of 7 or 8 photographers - who were positioned behind the wicket at our end to get the game winning bowler and batsman shots - were right in the firing line of the impending stampede and were likely to get overrun by the gathering hordes.

Our media supervisor then came up with the bright idea that we volunteers should go out and form a ring of steel around the photographers to keep the fans away from them and help avoid the risk of their camera equipment getting damaged in all the excitement.

This sort of thing wouldn't be allowed today - what with all the heightened awareness of Health and Safety requirements, insurance issues and so on – but we merry band of assorted students and other randomly recruited individuals, completely untrained and inexperienced in terms of security or crowd control, were marched out through the cordon onto the area around the pitch where the photographers were gathered and stood there looking a rather unlikely line of riot police, albeit without the benefit of protective gear or batons.

With self preservation figuring quite highly on my own personal list of priorities, I felt especially vulnerable as, while everybody else had their media centre uniform of Cricket World Cup t-shirts and hoodies on, mine didn't fit me properly so I was standing out like a sore thumb in a yellow weatherproof jacket and – despite my best efforts not to – distinctly looking as if I was in charge...

With just two balls left in the game Akram bowled McGrath out for a duck. The Australian innings was over, Pakistan had won and the fans went wild.

Rather like when you are messing about in the sea on holiday and an extra big wave comes along and crashes over your head, I think we probably all shut our eyes and clinched up ready for the onslaught of excited cricket fans who – luckily, as it happened - didn't overrun our plucky photographers position and went respectfully round us on their way onto the pitch.

So, the threat to life and limb all over and done with, the players and officials retired to the stand for the post match interviews and presentations and we eventually made our way back to the media centre to do media centre type things for a bit.

We got stuck in a huge traffic jam coming away from Headingley on the way home but it was quite a nice late spring evening and we ended up taking the scenic route back to Preston via Keighley, Skipton and so on to give us time to come back down to earth after the day's exciting events.

There were three World Cup games held at Headingley in total and we were originally pencilled in to help out at all three. As well as the group game that we went to, they also hosted two games in the Super 6 round:

6th June: Zimbabwe v New Zealand
13th June – South Africa v Australia

But because they was a bit of a surfeit of volunteers at the first game, and not enough meaningful tasks to give everybody something engaging to do (barring riot control duties, obviously ...) we were asked if we'd mind not going to the other Headingley matches.

That didn't really bother me to be honest as it was quite a trek from Preston where we living at the time and we were expected to get there at 6.30am to help get things ready for the day's game.

Adding on a good hour or so to get there - and needing time to get up and get ready - made it a very long day indeed, so we readily agreed to help them out on that score and decided we'd just content ourselves with the games at Old Trafford - which was a bit easier to get to...

LAYOUT FOR HEADINGLEY

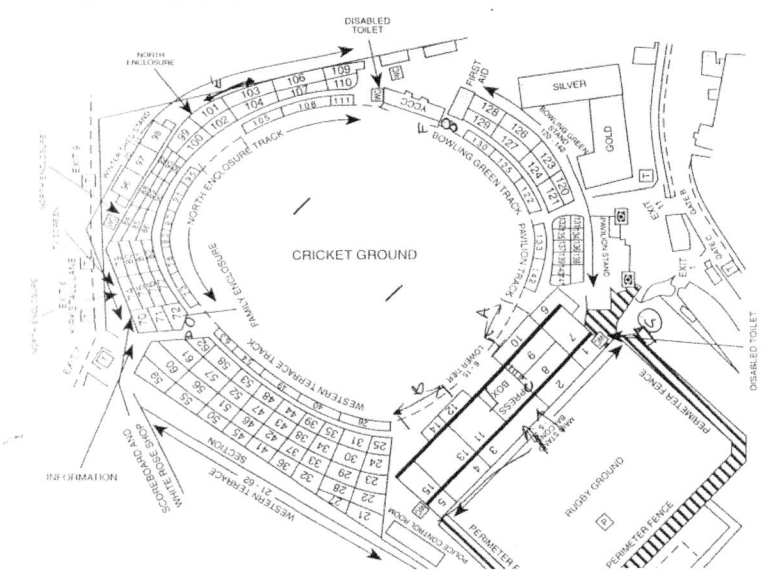

Copy of a Media Centre hand of the Headingley stadium layout. This one is marked up in biro with photographers' positions.

Newspaper graphic from the Daily Mail showing all the teams in the 1999 Cricket World Cup. Reproduced for illustrative purposes only - all rights reserved to the originators, obviously

23rd May 1999 – ICC World Cup, Headingley, Leeds
Pakistan 275/8 – Australia 265 (49.5 ov)
Pakistan won by 10 runs

Pakistan Batting		R	B	M	4s	6s
Wajahatullah Wasti	c SR Waugh b McGrath	9	31	47	1	0
Saeed Anwar	c †Gilchrist b Reiffel	25	23	32	5	0
Abdul Razzaq	c Fleming b Warne	60	99	126	3	1
Ijaz Ahmed	lbw b Fleming	0	6	6	0	0
Inzamam-ul-Haq	run out (Fleming)	81	104	131	6	1
Mohammad Yousuf	run out (Warne/Lehmann)	29	16	17	4	1
Wasim Akram (c)	c †Gilchrist b Fleming	13	12	22	1	0
Moin Khan †	not out	31	12	20	2	3
Azhar Mahmood	run out (Martyn/McGrath)	1	1	2	0	0
Saqlain Mushtaq	not out	0	0	3	0	0
Extras	(b 1, lb 5, nb 5, w 15)	26				
TOTAL	(50 Ov, RR: 5.50)	275/8				

Did not bat: Shoaib Akhtar. Fall of wickets: 1-32 (Saeed Anwar, 7.4 ov), 2-44 (Wajahatullah Wasti, 11.1 ov), 3-46 (Ijaz Ahmed, 12.3 ov), 4-164 (Abdul Razzaq, 39.3 ov), 5-216 (Mohammad Yousuf, 44.4 ov), 6-230 (Inzamam-ul-Haq, 46.2 ov), 7-262 (Wasim Akram, 48.6 ov), 8-265 (Azhar Mahmood, 49.3 ov)

Australia Bowling	O	M	R	W	ECON	WD	NB
Damien Fleming	10	3	37	2	3.7	4	1
Paul Reiffel	10	1	49	1	4.9	4	1
Glenn McGrath	10	1	54	1	5.4	4	1
Shane Warne	10	0	50	1	5	1	0
Steve Waugh	6	0	37	0	6.16	1	0
Damien Martyn	2	0	25	0	12.5	0	1
Darren Lehmann	2	0	17	0	8.5	0	0

Australia Batting		R	B	M	4s	6s
Adam Gilchrist †	b Wasim Akram	0	3	2	0	0
Mark Waugh	c †Moin Khan b Abdul Razzaq	41	49	74	6	0
Ricky Ponting	c Saeed Anwar b Saqlain Mushtaq	47	60	82	7	0
Darren Lehmann	c †Moin Khan b Saqlain Mushtaq	5	9	12	1	0
Steve Waugh (c)	b Shoaib Akhtar	49	65	122	2	1
Michael Bevan	c Ijaz Ahmed b Wasim Akram	61	80	102	3	1
Damien Martyn	b Wasim Akram	18	25	49	0	0
Shane Warne	run out (Ijaz Ahmed)	1	6	11	0	0
Paul Reiffel	c Wasim Akram b Saqlain Mushtaq	1	4	5	0	0
Damien Fleming	not out	4	3	15	0	0
Glenn McGrath	b Wasim Akram	0	2	1	0	0
Extras	(b 7, lb 10, nb 7, w 14)	38				
TOTAL	(49.5 Ov, RR: 5.31)	265				

Fall of wickets: 1-0 (Adam Gilchrist, 0.3 ov), 2-91 (Mark Waugh, 16.6 ov), 3-100 (Ricky Ponting, 19.2 ov), 4-101 (Darren Lehmann, 19.4 ov), 5-214 (Michael Bevan, 41.3 ov), 6-238 (Steve Waugh, 44.5 ov), 7-248 (Shane Warne, 46.2 ov), 8-251 (Paul Reiffel, 47.2 ov), 9-265 (Damien Martyn, 49.3 ov), 10-265 (Glenn McGrath, 49.5 ov)

Pakistan Bowling	O	M	R	W	ECON	WD	NB
Wasim Akram	9.5	1	40	4	4.06	1	5
Shoaib Akhtar	10	0	46	1	4.59	3	0
Azhar Mahmood	10	0	61	0	6.1	3	0
Saqlain Mushtaq	10	1	51	3	5.09	0	2
Abdul Razzaq	10	0	50	1	5	5	0

Above: Michael Bevan fielding for Australia during their World Cup game against Pakistan at Headingley (Photo by Paul Breeze)

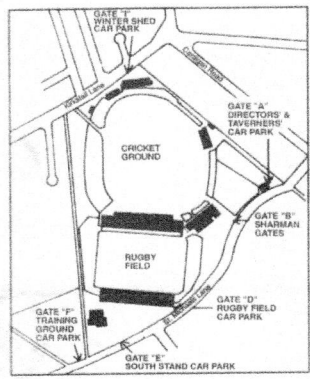

Car Parks:- Gate "A" – Blue; Gate "D" – Pink;
Gate "E" – Green; Gate "F" – Yellow; Gate"I" – Red

This ticket admits one car on condition that the
Leeds C. F. & A. Company Ltd. is not liable for any
loss or damage to car, passenger or contents. The
person holding this ticket is deemed to accept the
above condition, and no car can be otherwise
admitted. Should it be necessary because of
adverse weather conditions to close parking areas,
Leeds C. F. & A. Company Ltd. will use their best
endeavours to provide alternative parking.

£10.00 incl. V.A.T.

Nº 0105

AUSTRALIA v PAKISTAN

SUNDAY, 23rd MAY, 1999

TRAINING GROUND
RESERVED CAR PARK

ENTRANCE - GATE "F"
ST. MICHAEL'S LANE

No Coaches or Minibuses Allowed   Cars must not be left Parked Overnight

Top Left: front cover of the match programme for the Australia v Pakistan game
Top Right: Car parking information for CWC games at Headingley
Bottom: Car Park ticket for the Australia v Pakistan game

Lucy watching the Australian team warm up at Old Trafford before the game against the West Indies (Photo by Paul Breeze)

30th May 1999 – West Indies v Australia at Old Trafford.

The second game that we attended at the Cricket World Cup should have been an absolute cracker – West Indies v Australia but in the end it was a bit of a disappointment - certainly compared with the thrills and spills of the Pakistan game.

It was overcast for much of the day and play was stopped by showers on several occasions. This saw us - and thousands of bedraggled spectators - milling around the covered walkways behind the stands in search of somewhere dry to wait until the weather cleared. Luckily, unlike the rest of the spectators, we were at least able to take refuge in the media centre.

Something odd had happened with the ticketing at this game and the press (overspill) area that I managed to get us assigned to was right at the top of the members Pavilion building – that's the old fashioned red brick building that has since been modernised. It now has two extra floors with hospitality areas and balconies built across the top but when we were there, the top floor between the two towers was open to the elements with just the back few rows of seats covered by a roof.

The back rows of this top stand had been fitted with writing desks and power points so that any additional journalists who couldn't fit into the main press area would have somewhere to work from.

But it turned out that some fans had been sold tickets for those rows and kept wanting to sit there so I had to get the media centre manager to contact the box office and find out what was going on. Apparently, there had been a mix up with the Row numbers and some tickets had been issued to members of the public for the area that was now full of press desks. Thinking on my feet, I decided to quickly re-label one of the other rows - S or whatever it might have been - as X or Y or whatever the row in question was and explain this to the Steward who was on duty.

He said that it was normally a "members only" area up there (Lancashire County Cricket Club members) and, as he would probably know everybody anyway so there wouldn't be any problem.

However, it soon became clear that it wasn't, in fact, mainly LCCC members who were coming up to occupy those seats but members of the general public who had been allocated them via some sort of lottery and there were people with all sorts of bags and flags and picnic hampers - which our friendly steward found a little vulgar for "his" members area...

The game itself was actually less memorable than all the shenanigans with the crowd off it. The West Indies batted first and opener Sherwin Campbell was caught for 2 from just 14 balls. Jimmy Adam then went for a duck and the Windies were 7 for 2 halfway through the 5th over.

World batting record holder Brian Lara came in next – team captain and the man everybody wanted to see – but he was bowled by

Glenn McGrath for just 9 runs off 15 balls. After just 8 overs bowled, the match was already effectively finished as a sporting contest.

Shivnarine Chanderpaul did slightly better – managing to stay in for 38 balls and adding 16 to the scoreboard while, up the other end, the other surviving opener Ridley Jacobs was putting in a valiant display in the face of his team-mates' disappointing performances.

In fact, people were still coming in and taking their seats and saying how much they were looking forward to seeing Brian Lara bat later on – and I had to disappoint them by telling them that he had already been and gone...

Once Chanderpaul had gone, the rest of the Windies batting was extremely disappointing and we saw Stuart Williams go for 3, Phil Simmons for 1, Curtly Ambrose for 1, Mervyn Dillon for 0, Reon King for 1 and Courtney Walsh for 6. "Extras" (3 leg bys, 1 no ball and 18 wides) was actually the second highest contributor to the West Indies total with 22!

The only good thing about the innings was that opener Ridley Jacobs hit a decent enough 49 and made history by being the first ever cricketer to carry his bat (ie stay on from start to finish and remain not out at the end) in a World Cup match.

The West Insides were all out for a paltry 110 - with McGrath taking 5 wickets for just 14 runs and Shane Warne chipping in with 3 for 11. The most surprising thing about the morning's cricket was that they somehow managed to keep this dire display going for 46 overs before finally being bowled out!

We went and had our lunch in the Media Centre and when Lucy and I returned to the Press Overspill Area, we discovered that some of the members of the public had decided to go and sit in our media area to avoid the showers and were eating their sandwiches on our desks.

There were no journalists there to disturb as none had come up there all day. Too many stairs and too far from the hospitality goodies, I would expect... It had been rumoured that Dwight Yorke –

the Trinidadian football player who was with Manchester United at the time – might be coming to sit in our area but we only ever saw him down on the pitch chatting to the West Indies players during the warm up.

In fact, the only vaguely interesting person that we saw all day was Wilf McGuinness, the former United manager, who was quietly watching the match with some friends.

The Australian innings caused some controversy. They only needed 111 to win the game and qualify for the Super 6 round of the competition and, while they could probably have achieved this very quickly and easily, instead they chose to drag the game out as long as possible.

This was all to do with the Net Run Rate, ie how quickly they scored runs over the course of the games, and this would be used to decide which team would occupy which position in the final group table if more than one team finished on the same number of points.

With three teams ending up with 3 wins and 2 losses from their 5 group games, this became very important and, apparently (although I never fully understood the mechanics of it...), by somewhat cynically "managing" their run rate in this match, Australia

By ensuing that they ended up with a lower NRR than Pakistan, who ended up with 3 wins and two defeats from their 5 group games, Australia were able to make sure that they finished second in the group with the same won/lost record but an inferior NRR - and got an easier route in the next round of the competition.

Needless to say, most of the (non Australian) cricketing fraternity thought that this simply "wasn't cricket " – although it was completely within the rules.

Aussie opener Mark Waugh was caught behind for an uncharacteristically poor 3 after facing just 5 balls and Australia were 10 to 1 – but still very much in driving seat and ,by the time opener / wicket keeper Adam Gilchrist lost the second wicket in the 10th over, at 43-2 were well on their way to the target.

Darren Lehmann went for 9 off 13 balls in the 17th over with the score at 53/3 and then Ricky Ponting was dismissed for 20 at 62/4.

The game was interrupted by numerous rain breaks and Steve Waugh and Michael Bevan did not endear themselves to the crowd by taking an age to knock off the remaining 39 runs required to win the match.

So there you go – a rather disappointing and un-entertaining game, but it was still a World Cup Cricket match and we did get to see all of those world class players out on the pitch...

There were two more World Cup matches held at Old Trafford:

8th June India v Pakistan – Super 6
16th June New Zealand v Pakistan – Semi Final

which we were supposed to go and help at but, unfortunately, I had a minor health problem at the time and was given a course of anti-biotics to take.

I was perfectly all right and capable of doing my job properly but there was a chance that the tablets might cause stomach upsets and I was under instructions to avoid too much sunlight so I decided that being stuck indoors at the cricket wouldn't really be too much fun so we decided not to go.

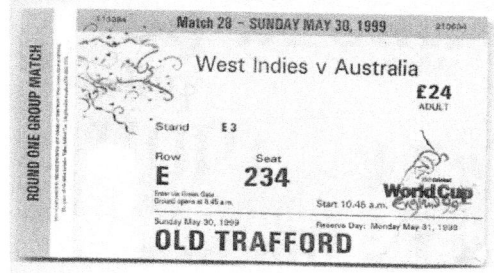

Ticket for the Australia v West Indies game at Old Trafford

The view of the match from our Press Overspill area (photo by Paul Breeze)

Post Match presentations on our balcony (Photo by Paul Breeze)

30th May 1999 – ICC World Cup , Old Trafford, Manchester

West Indies 110 – Australia 111/4 (40.4 ov)
Australia won by 6 wickets (with 56 balls remaining)

West Indies Batting		R	B	M	4s	6s
Sherwin Campbell	c ME Waugh b McGrath	2	14	19	0	0
Ridley Jacobs †	not out	49	142	197	3	0
Jimmy Adams	lbw b McGrath	0	1	1	0	0
Brian Lara (c)	b McGrath	9	15	14	1	0
Shivnarine Chanderpaul	b Warne	16	38	60	0	0
Stuart Williams	c ME Waugh b Moody	3	6	4	0	0
Phil Simmons	b Fleming	1	8	6	0	0
Curtly Ambrose	lbw b Warne	1	7	4	0	0
Mervyn Dillon	lbw b McGrath	0	9	11	0	0
Reon King	lbw b Warne	1	30	38	0	0
Courtney Walsh	b McGrath	6	11	23	1	0
Extras	(lb 3, nb 1, w 18)	22				
TOTAL	(46.4 Ov, RR: 2.35)	110				

Fall of wickets: 1-7 (Sherwin Campbell, 4.2 ov), 2-7 (Jimmy Adams, 4.3 ov), 3-20 (Brian Lara, 8.2 ov), 4-64 (Shivnarine Chanderpaul, 22.3 ov), 5-67 (Stuart Williams, 23.4 ov), 6-69 (Phil Simmons, 25.2 ov), 7-70 (Curtly Ambrose, 26.4 ov), 8-71 (Mervyn Dillon, 29.5 ov), 9-88 (Reon King, 40.5 ov), 10-110 (Courtney Walsh, 46.4 ov)

Australia Bowling	O	M	R	W	ECON	WD	NB
Glenn McGrath	8.4	3	14	5	1.61	0	0
Damien Fleming	7	1	12	1	1.71	2	0
Tom Moody	7	0	16	1	2.28	1	0
Brendon Julian	7	1	36	0	5.14	4	1
Shane Warne	10	4	11	3	1.1	1	0
Michael Bevan	7	0	18	0	2.57	5	0

Australia Batting		R	B	M	4s	6s
Adam Gilchrist †	b Ambrose	21	36	44	1	0
Mark Waugh	c †Jacobs b Ambrose	3	5	9	0	0
Ricky Ponting	c Chanderpaul b King	20	56	77	1	0
Darren Lehmann	c Adams b Ambrose	9	13	25	1	0
Steve Waugh (c)	not out	19	73	100	2	0
Michael Bevan	not out	20	69	85	2	0
Extras	(lb 4, nb 8, w 7)	19				
TOTAL	(40.4 Ov, RR: 2.72)	111/4				

Fall of wickets: 1-10 (Mark Waugh, 2.1 ov), 2-43 (Adam Gilchrist, 10.1 ov), 3-53 (Darren Lehmann, 16.2 ov), 4-62 (Ricky Ponting, 19.3 ov)
Did not bat: Tom Moody, Brendon Julian, Shane Warne, Damien Fleming, Glenn McGrath

West Indies Bowling	O	M	R	W	ECON	WD
Curtly Ambrose	10	0	31	3	3.1	1
Courtney Walsh	10	3	25	0	2.5	1
Mervyn Dillon	7.4	1	22	0	2.86	2
Reon King	10	2	27	1	2.7	1
Phil Simmons	3	2	2	0	0.66	2

Cricket World Cup 1999 – Final Standings

Group A	Pld	W	L	NR	T	NRR	Pts	PCF
South Africa	5	4	1	0	0	0.86	8	2
India	5	3	2	0	0	1.28	6	0
Zimbabwe	5	3	2	0	0	0.02	6	4
England	5	3	2	0	0	-0.33	6	N/A
Sri Lanka	5	2	3	0	0	-0.81	4	N/A
Kenya	5	0	5	0	0	-1.2	0	N/A

Group B	Pld	W	L	NR	T	NRR	Pts	PCF
Pakistan	5	4	1	0	0	0.51	8	4
Australia	5	3	2	0	0	0.73	6	0
New Zealand	5	3	2	0	0	0.58	6	2
West Indies	5	3	2	0	0	0.5	6	N/A
Bangladesh	5	2	3	0	0	-0.52	4	N/A
Scotland	5	0	5	0	0	-1.93	0	N/A

Super 6	Pld	W	L	NR	T	NRR	Pts	PCF
Pakistan	5	3	2	0	0	0.65	6	4
Australia	5	3	2	0	0	0.36	6	0
South Africa	5	3	2	0	0	0.17	6	2
New Zealand	5	2	2	1	0	-0.52	5	2
Zimbabwe	5	2	2	1	0	-0.79	5	4
India	5	1	4	0	0	-0.15	2	0

For the record, England dismally failed to qualify for the Super 6 round from their qualifying group and, after the next round of matches, the semi finals were:

16th June: New Zealand 241/7 – Pakistan 242/1 at Old Trafford
And
17th June: Australia 213 – South Africa 213 at Edgbaston

Anybody who saw it might remember that game at Edgbaston had a highly dramatic finale. The score was tied with 3 balls left to bowl and South Africa only needed one run to win their way through to the final.

There was a terrible mix up between batsmen Lance Klusener and Allan Donald that saw the latter run out to finish the game with both teams level on runs.

Because of the way that the tournament worked at that time it meant that Australia went through to the final due to a higher finishing position in the Super 6 round.

The final – held at Lord's - paired together Pakistan and Australia but anybody who was expecting a replay of the highly exciting group game that we had officiated at back at Headingley was in for a disappointment.

Pakistan were bowled out for just 132 from 39 overs and the Aussies knocked off the winning total of 133 in 20 overs for the loss of just two wickets to win the World Cup for the second time in its history.

Between the showers – lunch break at Old Trafford. You can just see the West Indies players on the pitch in the background (Photo by Posh Up North Publishing)

A Letter From Dickie Bird

During the summer of 2001, Lucy was taken ill and had to have a life-saving operation in hospital.

While she was there recovering, she started watching the live day time coverage of the England v Australia test matches on the TV in her room, which were still being shown live on Channel 4 in those days.

It surprised most of the nursing staff in good ole traditional East Lancashire that a woman might be interested in cricket.

In fact, Lucy often tells the story of when we were house hunting in Nelson and we were looking at the property that we eventually bought. She asked the (male) Estate Agent question a question about something or other and he sniffed, looked at her in a rather off manner, and then spoke to me with the answer. We noticed that sort of attitude quite a lot in that area at that time and found it rather quaint to be honest.

Anyway, after Lucy got home from hospital, we continued to watch the cricket every day over the rest of the summer as it gave her something to keep her occupied while she gradually built her strength back up after her operation.

We became very keen followers of the 5 day game and remain so to this day.

For Lucy's birthday, I bought her a copy of umpire Dickie Bird's autobiography – which I then rather un-chivalrously hogged and read from cover to cover before she could get a look in...

Towards the end of the book, Dickie wrote that he was always amazed and humbled at the amount of friendly letters that he continually received from all over the word and how he tried to reply to as many as he could.

He was also very impressed with the efforts of the Royal Mail as a great many of them were often simply addressed to "Dickie Bird, Cricket Umpire...." with nothing else on the envelope!

Encouraged by this information, I decided to write to everybody's favourite cricket umpire – adding some general notion of a postal address based on my gleanings from his book to tell him about how Lucy had benefited from watching the cricket during her recovery.

To my great surprise and delight I received a personal letter back from Dickie, which was really nice of him.

I can't reproduce it here as it is stashed away in a box somewhere, the result of one of our many house moves, but I can certainly tell you the gist of it.

He said that he was pleased that we had been enjoying watching the cricket and that it had helped Lucy recover from her operation. He also gave me a tongue in cheek admonishment for having hogged her book before she could read it - but he sent me a signed dedication that I could stick in the front ready for her to read it.

Even back in the days before I ever followed cricket, I always knew who Dickie Bird the umpire was - so this was really special and a very nice gesture from him.

Far Left: Dickie Bird's Autobiography which I would heartily recommend.

Left: Another collection of Dickie Bird's cricket memories that I hope to read in the future

Blackpool Cricket Club hosting a Lancashire v Middlesex county game in 2011 (Photo by LCCC Twitter)

Blackpool Cricket Club

Despite having got into following cricket in a big way when we were living in East Lancashire, we never really managed to go and watch any local games there on a regular basis.

The layout of most local league grounds is very much the same - with park benches around the perimeter, which are not especially comfortable to sit on for a long time so you have to take your own chairs with you.

Most spectators at this level tend to gravitate around the clubhouse and bar area and, to be fair, there is a nice modern club building at Nelson Cricket Club with a tidy / handy seating area immediately outside it but it is exposed to the direct sunlight and – on the few occasions when we went there, was full of people smoking.

When we moved to the Fylde Coast, being very particular about where we sat, we found similar accommodation issues at both St Annes and Lytham Cricket Clubs but were overjoyed when we happened upon Blackpool Cricket Club.

Blackpool is a much larger ground than a lot of the "village" type venues – with a 5000 capacity - and has rows of tiered seating along the front of the clubhouse and plenty of room for adjacent parking.

We discovered that a lot of people we know from non league football went to the cricket club so we both decided to join as members.

At the time that we first started going, they had an appeal to help pay for an extension to the changing rooms so we chipped in and when it was finished were invited to the opening evening and had our names inscribed on the subscribers board.

They had a large tv projector screen in the bar area and used to show live cricket and football on Sky Sports which was another bonus.

Back in the pre-covid period, Lucy and I always used to go to non-league football on a Saturday afternoon. When we lived in East Lancs, we would vary it between Nelson, Colne, Clitheroe or Padiham – depending on who was at home that day – and when we moved to Blackpool, we would go to Blackpool Mechanics, Squires Gate or Wren Rovers, which were close to where we lived - or occasionally Fleetwood, which was a bit further away.

As we had a nice routine worked out for a football Saturday, we would try and keep the same structure during the summer as well and just go to cricket instead of football.

The clever thing about going to the cricket was that, if the Blackpool 1st team were away, their 2nd team would generally play at home against the 2nd team of the same opposition meaning that there was a match on almost every Saturday through the summer months.

So we would go to Blackpool Cricket Club for the afternoon, watch the game for a couple of hours and maybe have a cup of tea and a scone in the club house. Having not been there for the toss or the start of play, it often took a little while to work out which team was batting but we just enjoyed watching the game and were never overly partisan about who we wanted to win.

Quite often the first innings would come to a close just at the time that we would be ready to leave so we would go at that point and never necessarily finding out what the result was....

Lancashire v Worcestershire - 2005

Lancashire usually play a county championship match at Blackpool once every summer and we went along to that on a couple of occasions. As the county game was scheduled for late August - coinciding with Lucy's birthday – we decided to treat ourselves and go for the hospitality package, which meant that we'd have our own seating on the top floor balcony of the pavilion along with lunch, tea and drinks throughout the day.

If I remember correctly, we went two years running to the County Game – for the first day against Worcestershire in 2005 and against Warwickshire in 2006.

When we were at the Blackpool Northern League game the weekend before the county game, we were impressed with all the preparations that were going on. Big marquees were being set up and all sorts of deliveries being made.

On the day itself we took a taxi to the ground as it would have been difficult to find anywhere to park without having to walk too far. It was a nice airy sunny day and a huge crowd had gathered for the game.

In fact, it was so sunny that they had to keep stopping play to get people to cover over shiny bits on their cars which were parked around the ground, the reflections of which were putting off the batsmen.

As I recall, most of the day's play revolved around Lancashire's Mal Loye who batted very well and reached the grand total of 187.

Jimmy Anderson was also in the Lancashire team but we didn't get to see him in action as Lancashire declared at 562/8 during the second day – before he needed to bat - and we were only there for the first day.

The Worcestershire team that fielded included Chris Gayle (the big hitting "Universe Boss" guy from the West Indies...) and England players Graeme Hick and Vikram Solanki.

For the record, Worcestershire managed 376 in their first innings and were forced to follow on. Their second innings collapsed and they were all out for 133 mid morning of the 4th day.

We did the same the following summer as well – ie watched cricket instead of football on Saturday afternoons – just going along to cheer on whoever happened to be playing that day.

The fascinating thing about the cricket club was, with it being so close to Blackpool's iconic Stanley Park, you'd get all sorts of people - other than cricket spectators coming to the clubhouse over the course of the day.

Stanley Park also has the town's athletics arena and is home to the Blackpool Stanley Rugby league club. There are also tennis courts, table tennis, football and hockey pitches, a skate park, bandstand, boating lake and nice areas to walk around.

The park hosts all sorts of large events right through the year from school sports days to classic car rallies and a lot of people from those events would end up at the cricket club house to have a drink and watch sports on the big screen.

What difference a decade makes... Lucy with the London charity hockey team at Blackpool Cricket Club in July 2010. Back in 2010, this would have been seen as humorous whereas now it would be thought of as rather offensive. (Photo by Paul Breeze)

In July 2010, we came across a group of guys in fancy dress who told us that they were a hockey team from London who were up for a weekend charity tournament at the park venue. They said that it was held every year and that all the teams came in costumes - and it was as much a social event as a sporting contest.

As I happened to have my sound gear with me, we recorded an interview with them for our Best Kept Secrets radio show on 103.2 Preston FM and you can still hear it today on our website.

Lancashire v Warwickshire - 2006

We had a day at the county match for Lucy's birthday again as well. This time it was Lancashire against Warwickshire but we didn't enjoy it quite so much.

Knowing our way round slightly better by then, we drove to the ground and parked in a side street across the road from the park, albeit a bit of a yomp from the main entrance.

The weather was overcast and the play kept getting interrupted by showers. In fact, the match was eventually rained off on the third day and declared a draw.

Lancashire had hit 456/9 (declared) over the first two days. They bowled Warwickshire out for 231 on the third day and then the weather set it and washed the game out after just 2 overs of their second innings.

Iain Sutcliffe did most of the damage for Lancashire with a knock of 159 while Aussie Stuart Law and New Zealander Nathan Astle chipped in with 61 and 64 respectively. The Warwickshire team had England players Jonathan Trott, Moeen Ali and Nick Knight in their line up - and they obviously spent the day that we were there in the field. Naqaash Tahir took 7 wickets for Warwickshire in what was otherwise a largely forgettable match.

From a slightly "gourmandise" point of view, it seemed as if somebody different did the catering this second year and we didn't enjoy the food as much. There also appeared to be more emphasis in the hospitality area on people drinking - and getting more and more beer - so the atmosphere wasn't as good as the previous year.

But it's certainly still worth going, if you have never been as it's a great experience - and I'm sure they will have put a lot of work into their hospitality packages in the intervening years.

Left: Paul with Beki Bondage at Blackpool Cricket Club in December 2011 (Photo by Lucy London) Right: Lucy with Paul Rooney from Vice Squad (Photo by Paul Breeze)

Vice Squad At Blackpool Cricket Club – 17th December 2011

When there is no cricket on at the cricket club, they hold other events like beer festivals and musical festivals outside in the summer months and a variety of other things indoors in the winter.

We attended a rather unusual non-cricket event there on 17th December 2011 when my all time favourite band Vice Squad (who I first saw play live in 1983) played a gig there.

Apparently there is a chap in Blackpool who is a big fan of the band and he sponsors them to travel up once a year to play at some venue or other in the town and, on this occasion, it was at the cricket club.

We saw posters in the clubhouse when we were at one of our Saturday games and made enquiries about tickets. It turned out that due to the regulations of the club, they weren't allowed to hold it as a private event for ticket holders and members had to be allowed access to the club at all times and, as club members, we were given free tickets to the gig.

We had been in contact with Paul and Beki from Vice Squad due to our radio shows on 103.2 Preston FM and had promoted their recent CD releases and done interviews with them so they knew who we were already and it was nice to meet up with them for a chat before the music started.

It was a bit of a surreal evening all round, to be honest as, before the gig we went to an ice hockey match at the SubZero rink in Cleveleys, then had a quick McDonalds tea on the way to the cricket club.

There were three local bands playing in support – Litterbug, One Way System and Pink Hearse and while all that was going on, Lucy suddenly got inspiration to write her Miss Blackpool song (which isn't in the least bit punk by the way,..)

She got talking to a young chap called Lee who had noticed her scribbling away and he told her that he recognised the signs of having to make notes whenever the muse grabs you as he was also a songwriter.

He actually then sat down there and then and composed a poem, which he then gave her and here it is:

When my heart is on my mind
I feel it all the time,
Slipping through my fingers
A heart full of Ninjas.
I will remember
December.

Lee. 17.12.2011, Blackpool Cricket Club

Me And Ian Botham - 20th March 1982

Football League Division 4 - Peterborough United 2- Scunthorpe United 1

Everybody loves Ian Botham – or Sir Ian Botham as he now is - and while he is best known for his performances on the cricket field, he was a fairly decent football player as well, playing to keep himself in shape between his cricketing commitments.

He played non league football on and off during the late 1970s and early 1980 for Yeovil Town and then in the 1981/82 season he made some appearances for Scunthorpe United in the Football League.

According to Wikipedia, Botham played 11 times in the league for Scunthorpe United - and I was lucky enough to be present at one of those games.

This was the first season that I started going to watch the mighty Posh as a season ticket holder. Me and a load of my friends from school – Paul Winskill, Alan Platt and Chris Lamb among others - all cashed in on the season ticket for kids for £10 offer. And it was a good time to start going as the team had a pretty positive season, just missing out on promotion right at the death.

Scunthorpe were not particularly good that season finishing second bottom of the 4th Division with just 9 wins from 46 games - and I'm pleased to say that this game wasn't one of them.

Botham made his full debut for "The Irons" (as Scunthorpe United are known – whoever came up with that nickname was probably NOT a cockney...) in a 7-2 hammering away at Wigan Athletic on 13th March and he also played in their away game at Peterborough the following Saturday.

Despite being there, I don't really remember anything much about the game. The excellent 11v11 website reminds me that Peterborough won 2-1 but it is quite a long time ago, so I can be excused not recalling every minute detail.

I certainly remember seeing Botham playing and I remember that the smattering of travelling fans spent most of the game singing things like "At Least He Plays For England...!" They also had a banner with some sort of Botham slogan on it that looked as if it had been painted on an old bed sheet.

According to the match programme, Botham played at number 9 in the centre forward position. I don't really remember him coming across as a potent strike force and figured, if anything, he was more of a solid midfielder.

He looked a bit chunkier than the other players (his nickname was "Beefy" after all...) and, while acknowledging that my own abilities at football and other sports are extremely limited, and not wishing to be critical or sacrilegious or disrespectful in any way, I would humbly suggest that, had Scunthorpe not been struggling at the bottom of the league - and had he not been a famous cricketer who wanted to play for them, then there is probably a good chance he might not have been in the team...

But that is just my personal point of view and, at the same time, I fully respect him for putting himself out when he could have been cosying up at home waiting for the cricket season to start - and for making 11 more Football League appearances than I ever will...

The match programme from the Peterborough v Scunthorpe game in 1982 when Ian Botham played.

Although I would have bought one at the time, this one isn't mine...

Stuart Latham

Book Review:

"An Alternative View Of The World Of Cricket"

By Stuart Latham

Published September 2021
ISBN: 9781838332877

Having just finished binge-reading all of Lynda La Plante's Anna Travis detective novels in the correct order (and been a bit annoyed at some unnecessary continuity inconsistencies in the last one when it referred back to an earlier case…) I thought I'd have a change of subject and read about the slightly less corpse-ridden world of cricket for a while.

And the right thing came along at exactly the right time as Stuart Latham has just published the most delightful book about that fascinating sport called "An Alternative View Of The World Of Cricket".

Now I ought to flag up here that I may be a little biased as I am friends with Stuart and we share a lot of sporting interest and we have collaborated on a few projects together in the past - but this book has really grabbed my attention and I am very much enjoying reading it.

It is written from a personal point of view – by which I don't mean it's all "me, me, me...!" all the way through – but the subject matter IS based around Stuart's own involvement in cricket at various levels and he writes about the clubs that he has been associated with, some of the famous players he has met and others who he has admired over the years - including Jack Russell, Bob Willis, Farouk Engineer, Chris Broad and Hansie Cronje, among others.

A good example of this is the somewhat humorous "Ian Botham sanitary bin" story which, in fact, reminded me that I once saw Botham playing league football for Scunthorpe United – which is a story which will have to wait until I produce my own, admittedly shorter, cricketing memoir at some time in the future...

Stuart also has some interesting family connections within cricket and is directly related - via a migrating ancestor - to the former New Zealand test and ODI player Rod Latham and his son Tom, who is the current international wicket keeper for the "Black Caps".

There is also an interesting section on the Hearne family from Chalfont, Buckinghamshire, from whom Stuart is descended and who produced a number of fine County and "All England" players in the Victorian era and beyond.

Stuart has written numerous books on many different and fascinating subjects, including ice hockey, rugby, motor racing and military history and you can find a complete list with order links on his sales website at: https://www.sandtsales.co.uk/online-shop

PART TWO: BASEBALL

In the previous volume of North / South Divide, I somewhat foolishly stated that nobody would ever write a book about my baseball career – not even me... But - guess what - I was absolutely wrong!

I had already done that myself back in 1995 when I published "Bobcats Review" which was the story of the Preston Bobcats baseball team's 1995 season in BBF Division 1 North – featuring yours truly as a player.

Having just come across an archived copy of what was my first ever written publication, I decided to reproduce it in full for the benefit of future generations.

And as I now have more baseball related material than I initially thought I had, guess what – I AM now writing a book about my involvement in baseball – well, half a book anyway.....

Baseball is, in fact, the only sport where I have ever been a properly registered player, competed in a league and also been a proper coach. I even notched up proper official playing stats - so I suppose it's an achievement that should be celebrated in some small way rather than being forgotten about.

Also, it does fit in with the North / South Divide theme. It turns out that – although I didn't know it when I was living down in Peterborough - the sport of Baseball in this country also operates – or at least it did back when I was playing it - in North and South conferences.

In fact there was a competitive team based in Whittlesey a few miles from where I grew up and which I never knew about.

My all time player stats (as far as I can remember) are 1 home run and one catch – both of which were probably flukes as I was always crap at batting, fielding and catching even with huge great glove on – so that was probably why I ended up writing about baseball rather than playing it.

There's a bit of a pattern emerging here, isn't there...?

Anyway, here's your opportunity to read all about it!

Top: PB batting for the Preston Bobcats at Moor Park against the Newark Giants
Bottom: an away game at Sheffield (both 1994).

Preston Bobcats – 1994 & 1995

I found out about baseball in the early 90s when my then girlfriend was studying Art & Design at the University of Central Lancashire's Harris Building in Preston.

One of the technicians in the art department was an elderly chap called Frank Caunce who had a lifelong obsession with the game and ran the Preston Bobcats league team and juniors.

I was encouraged to go down to one of the training sessions (Wednesday evenings during the spring / summer months) and discovered that there was a devoted core of local enthusiasts and that they trained and played their games at a marked out baseball diamond on Moor Park.

I was instantly welcomed by all, although to be honest I think they were always short of players so they would probably have welcomed just about anybody - and within a couple of weeks, I was playing my first game.

The first game I played in was against a team from Hessle in Hull and although, I wasn't properly registered with the league by then, I was still allowed to play as Preston were a player short and the Hull manager Kevin Macadam was one of the BBF league official and was able to give me a special dispensation.

Oddly enough, I did better in that first game than I ever did after actually getting the hang of it – too much thinking, I imagine.

Before the game, everybody said that if I managed to get a "hit" – which means to hit the ball and make it to first base – then that would be quite a good achievement for a first ever game.

In the event, I actually scored a run and caught somebody out - so was quite pleased with myself.

I trained and played on and off with the Bobcats for two seasons – summer 1994 and 1995.

And funnily enough, I picked up more injuries playing baseball – training at baseball, in fact, - than I ever did playing ice hockey. I damaged my right thumb when a two handed catch of a high ball went horribly wrong and plummeted embarrassingly at my feet in a practice session.

And then I broke a bone in my wrist and needed a plaster cast after a teammate pushed me over while I was attempting a home run in another such silly episode.

I got on well with the other players and I actually enjoyed the game even though I wasn't really much good at it.

BUT I was a lot better at it than people who had never played before.

Through my involvement with the Bobcats team I got involved with writing match reports for the local Preston Citizen newspaper, which I don't think exists anymore. That was the first time I had anything published anywhere and although the reports didn't have my name on them, it was still quite a thrill to see them in the paper every week.

At the end of the season, I gathered them all together and produced a souvenir booklet. The Bobcats actually finished second in the league that year and Frank gave us all a silver medal to celebrate the achievement.

In September 1995 I left my job and started studying full time at university in Preston. This, unfortunately, meant that I had to work at weekends to earn a bit of money and, as such, it wasn't feasible for me to play Sunday afternoon games with the Bobcats any more.

But I was – at least - able to continue my involvement with baseball in a few other interesting ways!

A **Posh Up North** **Publication**

Selling Price
£ 1.00
Where Purchased

Bobcats REVIEW

The 1995 Season
In BBF Division 1 North

Front cover of the original 1995 edition of "Bobcats Review"
The full publication is reproduced on the following pages.

Preston Bobcats Baseball Team

Team Honours:	1995 – BBF Division One Northern Conference
	1994 – Promoted From BBF Division 2 North
	1987 – Team Founded
Manager & Head Coach:	Frank Caunce
Press Officer:	Paul Breeze
Club Treasurer:	Simon Lesser
Field Coach:	Alan Milhench
Registered BBF Scorer:	Pauline Howarth
Registered BBF Coaches:	Frank Caunce & Peter Howarth
Home Ground:	Moor Park, Blackpool Road, Preston

History of The Club

Preston Bobcats baseball team was founded in 1987/88. Having played in the Merseyside League in the 1950s and formed a short-lived Leyland Tigers in 1954, I maintained interest in the game by organising softball at the Polytechnic – now University in Preston.

Sponsorship of the Federation in Britain in 1987 saw the founding of a national league of elite players and the publishing of a new magazine for baseball called "First Base".

As a result of correspondence in this magazine, I was able to re-establish contact with old colleagues from Merseyside who were still active in baseball and who encouraged me to try and form a team in Preston. After much advertising and not so gentle persuasion, this was achieved and we were welcomed, as complete novices, into the then North West League. A number of the original players are still with the team and are highly valued.

The British Baseball Federation undergoes almost annual transformation in its efforts to provide the best possible competition and Preston have so far coped well in adapting to the changes. We have achieved some kind of stability and have been able to attract players to the team regularly to compensate for the expected turnover each season. Long may it continue.

Frank Caunce, Team Manager

Views On The 1995 Season

A new season. First Division baseball. A chance to renew rivalry with Liverpool Tigers and Stretford As. A roster on 19 players – surely a record for the club – and lots to look forward to....

Then the Tigers drop out before the season gets underway. Very sad for a well established team. I hope they will regroup soon.

My hopes are that in this higher division we will play at least .5000 ball and give the other teams something to think about.

Very disappointing that some of the squad were never seen again after spring training and others seemed to lose interest after only a few games. A manager becomes perplexed when he gets no response to letters and phone calls – surely common courtesy requires a player to inform the team of his intentions.

In the event, responsibility fell on the same seven or eight players as before to carry us through and I cannot praise them enough especially those who do all the work at home games setting up and taking down the field equipment.

Thank you drivers who undertook long hauls to often poorly equipped venues in far off towns.

Thank you to Alan Milhench for coaching the team both on and off the field, to Pauline Howarth for scoring the games in sometimes awful weather and to Paul Breeze for his press reports and other work.

Congratulations to Damian Mullen and Anthony Howarth on being selected for England v Scotland. Welcome to David Farrar – an invaluable acquisition.

Thanks to all who contributed in their own particular way.

The 1995 Preston Bobcats Roster

Frank Caunce – Team Manager & Head Coach

Previous Clubs: Robins (M'side Lge) 1950-54, Leyland Tigers 1954, Founded Bobcats 1987/88

Hard working team manager and coach, also coaches juniors and various locals schools. Still plays occasionally for the team when not called upon to umpire

Steve Atack – 3rd Base / Short Stop

Previous Clubs: none

A founder member of the club and now in his 8th season. A good team leader and smart base runner.

Paul Breeze – Outfield

Previous Clubs: None

Now in his second season with the club, having made a late rookie start at the age of 27. A useful utility player as well as being team Press Officer

Barry Agnew – 2nd Base

Previous Clubs: Glasgow Diamonds, Sheffield Bladerunners, Yorkshire Yankees

Very experienced player who is a reliable hitter and base runner. Won the North West award for stolen bases in 1994.

David Farrar – Outfield

Previous Clubs: Ashfield Rangers / Hounslow

17 years experience with his previous club before becoming the Bobcats first big time signing of the year.

Can play in any position and is a solid backup catcher.

Pat Clugston – Outfield

Previous Clubs: Manchester Lions

Lively team player with great experience. Can play in all positions but excels in the outfield.

Peter Howarth – 1st Base

Previous Clubs: None

Very experienced player and assistant team coach with additional responsibilities with the junior team.

Regular first baseman but is also a meritable catcher.

Anthony Howarth – Pitcher /Infield

Previous Clubs: None

First choice pitcher and already in his 7th season with the club, having moved up through the junior ranks.

Recently made his international debut as was winning pitcher in an England win over Scotland. Excellent base hitter and run scorer and also plays middle infield.

Diana Howarth – Outfield

Previous Clubs: Panthers U16s

Distinguished career as junior player, including international duties. Made Northern Conference history this season by being the first lady to play in a senior fixture.

Don McNulty – Catcher

Previous Clubs: Southport Mets

With the club since its inception. First class catcher and experienced all round player. Not flashy but very consistent. Always at or near the top in fielding percentage

Laurent Lot – Infield

Previous Club: La Rochelle

Good acquisition with French league experience. Made a good contribution to the team effort during his short stay in England

Alan Milhench – Pitcher / Infield

Previous Clubs: Senators (Canada) and various community teams

Very experienced player as well as field team manager and coach. Good starting pitcher and all-rounder as well .

Damian Mullen – Outfield / Pitcher

Previous Clubs: Hemel Red Sox

Outstanding all round player who excels in the outfield and is our only left handed pitcher. Made his international debut for England this summer.

Peter Shone – Pitcher / Infield

Previous Clubs: None

Ferocious hitter who blends experience from his 8 years with the team with adaptability to play in most positions. Took a break last season but back with a vengeance this time around.

Mark Nickson – Outfield

Previous Clubs: None
In his 3rd season with the club. Good glove, but not always available

Simon Lesser – Pitcher / Outfield

Founder member of the club and club treasurer. Inactive this season due to illness and business pressures.

Alan Hobin – Outfield / 2nd Base

Previous Clubs: None

Has become a regular member of the team since making his debut last season.

Paul Hirst – Outfield

Previous Clubs: none
In his first season with the team.

Lee Robinson – Outfield

Previous Clubs: None
In his first season in the game.

Simon Thynne – Infield / Outfield

Previous Clubs: None
Made an impressive debut in his first season

The Bobcats 1995 Season At A Glance

Date	Home	Score	Away
7th May	Stretford As	25-13	Preston Bobcats
14th May	Preston Bobcats	15-14	Barnsley Strikers
21st May	Nottingham Pirates	24-14	Preston Bobcats
28th May	Preston Bobcats	11-12	Hull Royals
18th June	Preston Bobcats	9-5	Tamworth Strykers
2nd July	Preston Bobcats	12-13	Stretford As
9th July	Barnsley Strikers	25-14	Preston Bobcats
16th July	Preston Bobcats	9-0	Nottingham Pirates
6th August	Nottingham Pirates	0-9	Preston Bobcats
13th August	Hull Royals	9-21	Preston Bobcats
13th August	Preston Bobcats	8-9	Hull Royals
20th August	Preston Bobcats	9-0	Barnsley Strikers
27th August	Stretford As	15-16	Preston Bobcats
3rd September	Preston Bobcats	9-3	Tamworth Strykers
3rd September	Tamworth Strykers	15-3	Preston Bobcats

The BBF Division One Northern Conference for 1995 was scheduled to be played between 7 teams, ie: Stretford As, Preston Bobcats, Nottingham Pirates, Barnsley Strikers, Hull Royals, Tamworth Strykers and Liverpool Tigers, with each team playing each other home and away for a 12 match season.

The Liverpool team dropped out prior to the start of the season and the original schedule was left at 6 teams playing a 10 match season.

Midway through the season, the BBF decided that each team would play an additional round of games, mixed between home and away, for a revised season of 15 games in total.

Stretford As 23 – Preston Bobcats 13
Sunday 7th May 1995

The Preston Bobcats had a baptism of fire in their first BBF Division 1 North match of the season away at local rivals Stretford. This was the Bobcats' first game in the higher division, having been promoted from Division 2 last year.

The first inning ended scoreless, with both teams having difficulty mastering a poor quality pitch with unusually large pitcher's mound.

The breakthrough came in the second when Bobcats' new boys Simon Thynne and Paul Hirst both clocked up early runs – the latter having to flatten the Stretford catcher on the home plate to do so. This was followed up by runs for Steve Atack and Alan Milhench courtesy of a 2–base hit by Damian Mullen.

Stretford hit back, however, and ended the 2nd inning 8–4 up.

The game continued in pretty much the same vein, with Stretford outscoring the Bobcats in each of the subsequent innings – bar the 5th when Mullen brought in Alan Hobin and Steve Atack before having the favour repaid from the bat of Pete Howarth in a 5–4 inning.

The match finally came to a close at the end of the 7th inning when Stretford gained a 10 run lead, which automatically halts the game at that stage.

In all, a low key start in a new, higher division for the Preston team, but watch out for better things when they entertain the Barnsley Strikers at home on their Moor Park pitch next Sunday at 2pm.

Preston scorers in full: Milhench 3, Atack 3, Mullen 2, Hurst 2, Hobin 1, McNulty 1, Thynne 1.

Preston Bobcats 15 – Barnsley Strikers 14
Sunday 14th May 1995

The Preston Bobcats baseball team notched up their first BBF Division 1 points of the season with a closely fought victory over the Barnsley Strikers at Moor Park on Sunday.

Team skipper Alan Milhench led from the pitcher's mound as he struck out 3 Barnsley batters in the early innings as well as scoring 3 runs.

Damien Mullen demonstrated his all–round skills as he pitched 2 strike–outs and clocked up 3 runs, as well as making 2 important catches in the outfield whilst, in the infield, father and son duo Pete and Anthony Howarth combined well to run seven runners out at 1st base

It was all square after 2 innings but the Bobcats had pulled away into a 10–5 lead by the end of the 5th. Barnsley put up a brief struggle late on with three 3–run innings but weren't quite able to make up the deficit.

Pete Shone – back in the side after a year's layoff – acted as chief playmaker, batting in 5 other runners, as well as scoring himself.

The Bobcats will now be looking to build on this performance when they travel to Nottingham next Sunday.

Preston Team: Milhench (3), Mullen (3), McNulty (2), Shone, Thyne, Nixon, A Howarth, P Howarth, Agnew, Clugston (all 1), Breeze, Hobin

Nottingham Pirates 24 – Preston Bobcats 14
Sunday 21st May 1995

Local baseball team the Preston Bobcats were not able to build upon the previous weekend's league victory as they slumped to defeat after a spirited performance away at Nottingham on Sunday.

The Bobcats started well, keeping the score down to 2–2 after 2 innings and opened up a 6–4 lead by the end of the 3rd, only to have the home side fight back to make it all square at 10–10 at the end of the 5th.

Conditions, however, conspired against the Bobcats and the problems that they'd had all afternoon coming to terms with an exaggeratedly sloped playing surface came to a head as Nottingham took full advantage to storm into a 20–10 lead in the 6th inning. Preston responded well to claw 4 runs back, only to find themselves behind again to a match–winning 24–14 deficit at the end of the 7th.

For Preston, Laurent Lot and Simon Thynne lead the attack with 3 runs each and Mark Nickson was outstanding in the unfamiliar position of centre–field where he made 4 top class catches – including one spectacular diving effort.

Towards the end Diana Howarth made Northern Conference history as she became the first girl to play in a senior fixture.

The Bobcats will be hoping to maintain their unbeaten home record next Sunday when they entertain the Hull Royals on Moor Park – pitch off 2pm.

Preston Team: Atack, Lot, Thynne, P Howarth, Milhench, Hirst, Nickson, A Howarth, McNulty, D Howarth, Clugston, Hobin

Preston Bobcats 11 – Hull Royals 12
Sunday May 28th 1995

The Preston Bobcats lost out by a single, last gasp run in a thrilling encounter at home to high–flying Hull Royals on a windswept Moor Park on Sunday.

All had gone to plan early on as the local team managed to open up a 6–2 lead by the end of the 3rd inning and, in fact, succeded in keeping Hull scoreless for 6 of the total 9.

The visitors pulled 2 runs back in the 5th but runs from Anthony Howarth and Damian Mullen in the 8th looked to have put Preston into an unassailable 8–4 lead.

Hull came out to bat for the last time all fired up, needing to hit 5 runs to pull in front. In fact they hit 7, taking the lead for the first time and leaving the Bobcats having to score 3 themselves to tie the game or 4 to win.

A stirring fightback with runs from Simon Thynne, Pete Howarth and Anthony Howarth saw the score level at 11–11 at the end of the 9th inning requiring an extra inning to be played to decided the game. During this, Hull managed to score whilst Preston were unable to reply.

A faultless all round team performance was typified by Pete Howarth who played admirably as stand–in catcher and Anthony Howarth who had a good game at pitcher with 5 strike outs and 2 catches, as well as top scoring with 3 runs.

Preston team and scorers: A Howarth 3, P Howarth 2, Thynne 2, Atack/
Hobin/Clugston/Mullen (all 1), Agnew, Nickson, Breeze

Bobcats Baseball News
Sunday 4th June 1995

The Preston Bobcats have been taking full advantage of a break in their league schedule to prepare for their next BBF Division One North home match against the mid–table Tamworth Strykers at Moor Park on Sunday June 17th.

Tamworth were one of the pre–season favourites for promotion to the Premier Division but have recently suffered defeat at the hands of the Hull Royals – who also pipped the Bobcats in a thrilling extra–innings encounter – and a 9–0 reverse last weekend by Barnsley who Preston beat earlier in the season.

The Strykers visit is now keenly anticipated by the local team, who will be anxious to get back to winning ways having found themselves at the bottom of the league table after the weekend's other games.

BBF Division One North Table (as at 5th June 1995)

	Won	Lost
Hull Royals	3	1
Stretford As	2	1
Barnsley Strikers	2	1
Tamworth Strykers	1	2
Nottingham Pirates	1	2
Preston Bobcats	**1**	**3**

Bobcats Baseball News
Sunday 11th June 1995

A second consecutive weekend without a game has left the Preston Bobcats stuck at the foot of BBF Division One North.

The local team will be looking to get back to winning ways – and off the bottom of the division – at Moor Park on Sunday when they entertain fellow strugglers Tamworth Strykers who have, so far, been unable to live up to their pre–season billing of title favourites

The Bobcats have been boosted by the signing of 33–year old David Farrar from Premier Division side Hounslow Rangers who joined team training last weekend. Farrar brings with him over 15 years of experience and can play in any position, making him a valuable addition to the squad .

BBF Division One North Table (as at 12th June 1995)

	Won	Lost
Hull Royals	3	1
Stretford As	3	1
Barnsley Strikers	2	2
Nottingham Pirates	2	2
Tamworth Strykers	1	3
Preston Bobcats	**1**	**3**

Preston Bobcats 9 – Tamworth Strykers 5
Sunday18th June 1995

The Preston Bobcats lifted themselves off the bottom of the Division 1 North table wi
a well deserved victory over fellow strugglers Tamworth Strykers in a tense and
thrilling game at Moor Park on Sunday.

The first inning ended with the home side taking a close 3–2 lead with runs from Atac
Milhench and Mullen. This was followed by a tense, scoreless 2nd inning before runs
from Farrar, Mullen, Clugston and Atack made it 7–2 at the end of the 4th.

After a tactical fielding change, Farrar took over at catcher from McNulty, who
immediately went on to make an important catch in the outfield.

The Bobcats managed to keep the visitors scoreless for 6 of the 9 innings thanks to a
watertight fielding display by the whole team and solid pitching from Anthony
Howarth.

The Strykers rallied enthusiastically towards the end, scoring 3 more runs but were
unable to close the gap as scores by Milhench and McNulty ensured that the visitors
finished on the wrong end of a 9–5 scoreline.

The Bobcats have no game next weekend but play hosts to local rivals, the high flying
Stretford As on Sunday 2nd July.

Preston Team: Atack, Milhench, Farrar, Mullen, P Howarth, A Howarth, McNulty
                    Lot, Clugston, Hirst, Agnew, Breeze, Hobin

Preston Bobcats 12 – Stretford As 13
Sunday 2nd July 1995

The Preston Bobcats baseball team lost out to a last gasp burst by local rivals the Stretford As in a tense and thrilling, yet good natured, Division One North game at Moor Park on Sunday.

The Bobcats had lost 23 – 13 at Stretford in their opening game of the season but were hopeful of better things this time around and had been bolstered by a win over the A's in the North West trophy in May.

As it turned out, the home side played tremendously well as the scores see–sawed throughout the game and they found themselves leading their high flying visitors 10–9 going into the final inning. Stretford came out and scored 4 runs, leaving Preston needing four to win. Unfortunately, the Bobcats were only able to manage a further 2 and ended up on the wrong end of a 13–12 scoreline.

Top scorers for the Bobcats were Damien Mullen and Pete Howarth with 3 runs each and starting pitcher Alan Milhench contributed with a home run which also batted in two other runners.

The other Preston runs were scored by Agnew, Lot, Shone, Farrar and McNulty.

The Bobcats hit the road next Sunday for a match away at mid–table Barnsley Strikers, who they beat 15–14 at home earlier in the season.

Barnsley Strikers 25 – Preston Bobcats 14
Sunday July 9th 1995

Preston Bobcats baseball team slumped to their 3rd consecutive away defeat of the season away at mid–table rivals Barnsley on Sunday, despite having stormed into a 12–2 lead after 3 innings.

A timely change of pitcher by the home side made all the difference and the local side only managed 2 further runs in the rest of the game.

Barnsley struck back with 23 runs in the last 4 innings – including 9 in the 8th – to take the victory.

Preston switched pitching duties between Alan Milhench, Pete Shone and Damien Mullen but were unable to stem the flow and, unluckily, catcher Don McNulty was injured midway through and outfielder David Farrar stepped in to deputise.

Top scorers for the Bobcats were Atack and Mullen with 3 runs each. Pete Shone also starred with two 2–base hits which, on an official pitch, would have been home runs.

BBF Division One action returns to Moor Park this Sunday when the Bobcats entertain the Nottingham Pirates, who managed to concede 39 runs at home to Barnsley last weekend.

Preston team: Atack, Mullen, Shone, Farrar, Nickson, Howarth, Hobin, McNulty, Milhench, Hirst

England Call Up For Bobcats Stars
Weekend 15/16 July 1995

Two Preston Bobcats players have been selected for the England national baseball squad to play against Scotland in Perth on Sunday.

Damien Mullen and Anthony Howarth have caught the selector's eye, having both performed consistently well for the local team throughout the season.

Howarth is Bobcats main choice pitcher and can also play outfield, whilst Mullen is the star outfielder who can also pitch.

Because of the international match, there are no league games this weekend. The Bobcats next match will be a week on Sunday away at table topping Hull Royals who they narrowly lost out to in a thrilling home encounter earlier in the season.

The Bobcats notched up their 3rd league win of the season on Sunday without even hitting a ball as the Nottingham Pirates weren't able to travel, thus forfeiting the game by a 9–0 scoreline.

Due to poor weather conditions last week, the proposed visit by BBC Radio 5 to the Bobcats training session was postponed and was rescheduled for a few weeks time.

Scotland 13 – England 16
Sunday July 23rd 1995

Two Preston Bobcats players figured prominently as the England national baseball team gained a thrilling victory over Scotland in Perth on Sunday.

Newly capped Damien Mullen played for the whole 9 innings scoring 3 runs and making a superb throw from the outfield to the home plate to get a runner out at a crucial stage of the game.

Anthony Howarth, the youngest member of the squad, was brought on as pitcher in the 6th inning as the team were trailing 8–7 but went on to turn the game around for an England victory.

The game was played in the best of spirits with the scores remaining close throughout. Victory was only clinched in the very last inning when a player from Nottingham hit a grand slam home run, bringing in 3 other runners as well as scoring himself, to rapturous applause..

Inning Scores	1st	2nd	3rd	4th	5th	6th	7th	8th	9th	Res
England	0	0	0	3	4	2	1	2	4	16
Scotland	0	1	4	0	3	2	2	0	1	13

Because of the international match, there were no league games last weekend. The Bobcats next match will be on Sunday away at table topping Hull Royals who they narrowly lost out to in a thrilling home encounter earlier in the season.

Hull Royals v Preston Bobcats
Sunday 30th July 1995

The away game at Hull Royals scheduled for last weekend was rescheduled to 13th August when two games will now be played consecutively between the two sides in a *double header* encounter.

The free weekend gave the Bobcats an extra training session to enable them to prepare for the crucial trip next weekend to mid–table rivals Nottingham Pirates where they suffered a heavy defeat earlier in the season.

The game should be a cracker as Bobcats' international pitching star Anthony Howarth will come up against fellow England player, hard hitting Ashley Killgas who scored the winning grand slam home run against Scotland in the recent friendly match.

The local side will be boosted by news that first choice catcher Don McNulty is now fit again, having recovered from the injury that he sustained away at Barnsley a couple of weeks ago.

♣   ♦   ♥   ♠

The Bobcats were due to play hosts to a crew from BBC Radio 5 Live at their Moor Park training session on Tuesday evening.

The National radio station were recording material for their Straight Up programme to be broadcast at 7.30 pm on Saturday evening.

The visit had originally been scheduled a few weeks ago but had to be postponed due to bad weather.

The BBC Visits The Bobcats
Tuesday 1st August 1995

BBC Radio 5 Live dropped in on the Preston Bobcats baseball team's evening training session to record material for their Saturday evening Straight Up series.

The programme is presented by Andy Parsons and Henry Naylor who are travelling along an imaginary line drawn north to south across Britain. They stop and report upon items of interest that they come across and Moor Park must obviously have happened to fall in their path.

The reporters spent about two hours with the team, chatting with the players and interviewing head coach Frank Caunce who has been in the game in the North West for almost fifty years.

An impromptu friendly match was quickly organised to give the visitors an idea of how the game is played. Naylor impressed everyone by hitting a home run whilst Parsons made a stylish infeed catch.

The radio team now have to condense two hours worth of tape recordings into a few minutes of broadcast footage as each 30 minute programme features 3 or 4 different items.

The edition of the programme featuring the Bobcats will go out on air in a few weeks time – keep an eye on Ceefax page 658 for details!

Nottingham Pirates v Preston Bobcats
Sunday 6th August1995

Local baseball team the Preston Bobcats had a disappointing time as they travelled to Nottingham still in search of their first BBF Division One North away win of the season.

They arrived to find that no match officials had been appointed for the game and, as neither team had any spare players who could stand in, the game ended up having to be played as an exhibition/training session between two sides who could have both done with the points.

Despite the disappointment of a wasted journey, in some respects the postponement could be a blessing as the Bobcats were without first choice catcher Don McNulty and England international pitcher Anthony Howarth who was carrying an injury.

The game will now be rescheduled for later in the season.

Preston have struggled thus far this season – their first in the higher division, having won promotion from Division 2 North last year – and have only won 3 of ther 8 league matches to date, the last one ironically being 9–0 home win over Nottingham.

Team morale remains high, however, as the Bobcats are still managing to hover just one place above the single relegation spot which is currently occupied by the Tamworth Strykers, who have been woefully unable to live up to their pre–season billing of title favourites.

The Bobcats still have to play Tamworth twice in the league – once home and once away – and will obviously be hoping to pull away from a potential end of season relegation showdown.

The local side now have to raise themselves for next Sunday when they travel the length of the M62 away to table–topping Hull Royals where they will play a *double header* , comprising two games played back to back between the two teams, to make up for a missed fixture earlier in the season.

The Bobcats pushed the Humbersiders all the way in their last encounter, finally losing out by a single run in the last inning of a thrilling game, and may relish this opportunity to go one better this time around.

Points Shared At Hull After Away Triumph
Sunday 13th August 1995

The Preston Bobcats baseball team travelled to table topping Hull Royals on Sunday for a crucial *double header* encounter which would effectively make or break their season – two wins would lift them to mid-table safety whilst two defeats would pitch them into a grim end of season relegation battle with the Tamworth Strykers.

As it turned out, the spoils were shared as Preston stunned the opposition by winning the first game – their first away win of the season – and narrowly losing the second.

Pride has been restored to the local team who can now look forward to next weeks home game with Barnsley with renewed optimism.

Preston Bobcats v Barnsley Strikers
Sunday 20th August 1995

Bobcats keenly awaited home game against mid-table Barnsley strikers was called off at the last minute as the visitors found themselves unable to field a full team.

The Preston team had been hoping for an opportunity to build on last weeks away win over table topping Hull Royals but will now have to wait until their trip to local rivals – Manchester based Stretford As – next weekend to get back into league action.

The weekend's postponement does, however, have some consolation as Preston will probably be able to claim the league points for the game as it is unlikley that there will be time at the end of the season for the fixture to be rearranged.

Stretford As 15 – Preston Bobcats 16
Sunday August 27th 1995

Battling Bobcats baseball team withstood a fierce comeback by local rivals Stretford to come away with a last gasp victory in a stunning match on Sunday.

Preston – obviously still buoyant from their away win at champions–elect Hull Royals a fortnight ago – came out firing on all cylinders and managed to storm to an 11–4 lead by the end of the 7th inning – courtesy of the exploits of demon pitcher Pete Shone, who pitched a creditable 16 strike outs overall.

Three more runs in the 8th inning would have secured only the Bobcats' second away win of the season (under league rules, a 10 run margin automatically stops the game from the 7th inning onwards), however it all went horribly wrong as a close decision went the way of the hosts who then rallied to hit an incredible 7 runs to tie the game to which the Bobcats had no reply.

A nervy scoreless 9th inning followed, forcing the match into a sudden death extra session, during which the Bobcats outslugged the As 5–4 to record an important victory.

Top run scorer for Preston was David Farrar with 4, followed closely by Pete Howarth with 3. Junior team player Chris Addison made his second appearance for the senior team and managed to get a base–hit.

The win was significant as the Bobcats now move above Stretford in the league table and look set to finish in a comfortable mid–table position in this, their first season at the higher level, having won promotion last time around.

Bottom placed Tamworth Strykers provide the opposition for the Bobcats' next league game at Moor Park on Sunday – pitch off 2pm.

Preston Scorers In Full: Farrar 4, P Howarth 3, Milhench/Shone/A Howarth/
                          Hobin all 2, Atack 1

Preston Bobcats v Tamworth Strykers - Double Header
Sunday 3rd September 1995

The Preston Bobcats finished their league season with a win and a defeat in a keenly contested double header encounter with Tamworth Strykers (2 x 5 inning games to make up for a missed date earlier in the season) at Moor Park on Sunday.

1st Game: Preston 9 - Tamworth 3

Preston took the lead in the first inning, scoring 4 runs through Howarth, McNulty, Mullen and Shone and assisted by some shoddy defensive play by the visitors as two of the runs came from fielding errors.

A tight defence by the home side - led by pitcher Shone with 4 strike-outs - kept the visitors scoreless for 2 of the 5 innings and down to 1 run in each of the other 3.

The game was niggly all the way through - as had been the case in the game between the two side earlier in the season - and threatened to blow out of control as the Strykers verbally contested every decision and the Bobcats found themselves on the wrong end of several seemingly clear-cut umpiring decisions:

Paul Breeze seemed to have been hit by a pitch during his first time at bat, which normally gives a batter a free walk to first base, but, on this occasion, no walk was awarded and shortly afterwards, Anthony Howarth was called out at 1st base when he looked to be well clear.

The middle innings of the game were tense - the second ending 0-1 to Tamworth and the 3rd 1-0 to Preston from a Pete Shone run, courtesy of another Strykers error.

Tamworth looked dangerous at times but failed to hit back and Preston made certain of the win with 4 more runs in the last inning from Hobin, Howarth, McNulty and Farrar.

Preston v Tamworth- Double Header (Cont'd....)

2nd Game: Preston 13 - Tamworth 15

The second game, with the Bobcats playing as the away team, looked as if it would go the same way as the Preston took a 5-1 first inning lead, with Pete Shone and Paul Breeze acting as chief playmakers, each batting in 2 runners.

The day had started badly for England international outfielder, Damien Mullen, who had suffered his first strike-outs of the season in the first game and it got worse in the second as he was hit twice by the ball as he stood at bat. Under the rules of the game, the Pitcher could have been expelled from the game but , as it was, he wasn't even spoken to by the Umpire, although Mullen did get a walk to first base each time.

He then went on to further make up for his misfortune by ending up as top scorer in the second game with 4 runs (5 overall in two games).

The turning point of the game came in the 3rd inning when the Bobcats failed to score and the Strykers hit 5 to take the lead.

The Preston side had up to now used 3 different pitchers in the second game: Mullen, Milhench and England pitching star Anthony Howarth. They then went on to make wholesale changes, bringing Pete Shone back to pitch, David Farrar taking over at catcher from Don McNulty, who moved to 3rd base and Howarth moving to 2nd base, but were still unable to prevent the Strykers notching up another 5 to give a total of 15.

Bobcats, with 11 runs from their 4 innings needed to score at least 4 in the 5th to force the visitors to bat again but only managed 2, from McNulty (Mullen) and Mullen himself (P Howarth), thus handing Tamworth a not-particularly-deserved 15-13 victory.

The afternoon's events leave the Bobcats with a final league record of Played 15, Won 7, Lost 8 and should leave them in a comfortable mid-table position, although a number of games to be made up by other teams will need to be played before the final league standings are known.

Final League Standings For BBF Division 1 North - 1995

The Preston Bobcats were handed second place in the league table in dramatic fashion as their topsy-turvy first season in Division 1 came to a close this weekend.

There was still one game still to play – a visit to Nottingham rescheduled from earlier in the season – and it looked as if the Bobcats would have to forfeit as not enough players would have been available for the trip, the season having already gone on longer than originally expected.

Conceding the game would have left the local side in a 3-way tie for 2nd place along with Stretford and Tamworth with each team having seven wins and eight defeats. However, Nottingham – already adrift at the foot of the table – forfeited the game, handing the Bobcats second spot in their own right with a revised record of 8 and 7.

The Bobcats season started badly with them occupying bottom spot for much of the early part of the season. However, an upturn in form midway through, as well as important away wins at champions Hull and local rivals Stretford, saw fortunes improve and the team end up in a league position that many might have thought unlikely at the start of the season considering the quality of the opposition.

All credit to the Preston side who have overcome all manner of adversity this season to finish in their highest ever league position. They now take a well earned break and can look forward to next season with optimism, knowing that they have proved themselves at the higher level.

Final Table:

Pos.	Team	Won	Lost
1st	Hull Royals	13	2
2nd	*Preston Bobcats*	8	7
3rd	Stretford As	7	8
4th	Tamworth Strykers	7	8
5th	Barnsley Strikers	6	9
6th	Nottingham Pirates	4	11

Hull Royals are promoted to Premier Division & Nottingham Pirates relegated to Division 2. Subject to any change in the league format, Bobcats will play in Division 1 (N) next season.

Games	Position	Player	At Bat	Hits	2 Base	3 Base	Home Run	Runs	RBI	Strikeout	How to Reach	Stolen Base	Out Stealing	Hit by Pitch	Sacrifice	Batting Avg	Put Outs	Assists	Errors	%
10	8, 6	Damian Mullen	40	24	4	0	3	27	18	2	5	22	0	2	0	.600	14	11	3	892
8	9,8,7	Peter Shone	34	17	5	1	0	12	15	1	3	10	4	1	0	.500	4	8	4	750
11	1,4,2,6,9,7	Alan Milbench	43	20	2	0	1	18	11	0	4	3	1	1	0	.465	6	21	4	870
11	4,6,1,8	Anthony Howarth	35	16	4	2	0	12	15	5	8	20	3	0	0	.457	12	28	6	869
5	9,6,5,7	Simon Thyme	23	9	5	0	0	7	4	4	1	4	0	1	0	.391	1	1	4	333
12	3,2	Peter Howarth	46	17	1	0	0	14	13	4	9	11	3	0	1	.369	107	3	4	973
10	5,3,6,2	Steve Atack	53	19	1	1	0	12	5	4	2	9	1	0	1	.358	23	11	5	871
10	2,7,9,5	Don McNulty	34	12	1	1	0	15	8	3	9	17	1	0	1	.352	44	5	4	924
8	7,2,6,5	David Farrar	30	10	2	0	0	16	8	4	7	7	0	0	0	.333	31	8	4	906
7	4,7,9	Alan Hobin	24	6	1	0	0	7	4	10	4	3	2	0	0	.250	4	3	5	583
4	7,8	Mark Nickson	21	5	1	0	0	3	5	3	0	1	1	0	0	.258	8	0	0	1000
7	7,9,5,4	Pat Clugston	22	5	1	0	0	3	5	3	0	1	1	1	0	.227	3	8	2	846
3	6,4	Barry Agnew	9	3	0	0	0	2	2	4	2	3	0	0	0	.333	4	8	3	800
2	7	Paul Breeze	3	1	0	0	0	0	2	0	0	0	0	0	0	.333	–	–	–	0
–	4,3,1	Laurent Lot	11	3	1	0	0	4	0	2	2	2	0	1	0	.272	–	3	1	916
6	7,5,9	Paul Hirst	10	1	0	0	0	3	2	2	3	1	0	0	0	.100	8	0	4	200
3	7,9	Chris Addison	10	1	0	0	0	0	2	6	0	0	0	0	0	.100	1	1	–	0
1	9	Diana Howarth	1	0	0	0	0	0	0	0	0	0	0	0	0	.000	–	1	–	0

Pitcher	Inns Pitched	Runs Faced	Hits Allowed	Runs Allowed	Earned Runs	Strike Outs	Base on Balls	Hit by Pitch	Balks	Balls Pitch	Decisions	Win	Loss	Run Ave
Milbench	23	126	40	34	24	6	9	0	0	1	1	1	0	9.39
A Howarth	28	152	39	49	31	16	19	0	4	0	1	4	2	9.96
Shone	26	147	45	44	32	27	23	1	1	0	2	2	0	11.07
Mullen	15	98	37	36	23	7	12	1	0	0	1	1	1	13.8
Lot	0.3	10	3	9	8	0	5	0	0	0	0	0	1	218

What The Papers Said.......

Baptism of fire for Bobcats

Preston Citizen - 11-5-95

STRETFORD A 23
PRESTON BOBCATS 13

PRESTON Bobcats had a baseball baptism of fire in their first BBF Division 1 North match of the season.

This was Bobcats' first game in the higher division, having been promoted from Division 2 last year. The first innings ended scoreless, with both teams having difficulty mastering a poor quality pitch with an unusually large pitcher's mound.

The breakthrough came in the second when Bobcats new boys Simon Thynne and Paul Hurst both clocked up runs.

This was followed up by runs for Steve Atack and Alan Millhench courtesy of a two-base hit by Damien Mullen. However, Stretford hit back and ended the second innings 8-4 up. The game continued in pretty much the same vein, with Stretford outscoring the Bobcats in each of the subsequent innings — bar the fifth when Mullen brought in Alan Hobing and Steve Atack before having the favour repaid from the bat of Pete Howart in a 5-4 innings.

The match finally came to a close at the end of the seventh innings when at Stretford gained a 10-run lead, which automatically ended the game.

Preston are looking to improve when they entertain the Barnsley Strykers at home on their Moor Park pitch on Sunday at 2pm.

Preston scorers were Millhench (3), Atack (3), Mullen (2), Hurst (2), Howart, McNulty and Thynne.

BASEBALL

Trojans win VE Day tournament

Sefton Trojans won the VE Day baseball tournament for the North West Cup at Bootle Stadium on Monday, beating the holders, Stretford As and Preston Bobcats in their two games.

Despite the chilly, windy weather Trojans immediately showed their batting strength in their first game which was against Stretford, with lead-off batter, outfielder Bob Orme, hitting an 'inside the park' home run.

Behind the controlled pitching of Peter Sharpe Trojans moved steadily ahead in each inning, going into the last leading 7-1, and a collapse in Stretford's fielding saw them romp away with five more runs in the last inning, to which their opponents could reply with only one, leaving Trojans 12-2 winners. Peter Sharpe was winning pitcher.

The second game saw Bobcats beat Stretford by a big margin, 24-7, avenging a defeat by them in a Northern Conference game the previous day. Stretford's pitching aagain crumbled in the later inings, and Preston had the winning pitcher in young Tony Howarth.

The decider saw Preston experience the full power of Trojans' batting, outfielder Rob Nesbitt hitting a home run and Bob Orme a treble and a double, while third baseman Ian Parker, catcher Steve Williams and short stop Mike Livingston all hit doubles.

Trojans won 15-0, with Martin Godsall registering his fourth win of the season.

● The next game is this Sunday, when Hull Warriors are the visitors to Bootle Stadium, pitch-off 1pm.

NORMAN WELLS

Good start, but Bobcats fail to master pitch

Preston Citizen 25-5-95

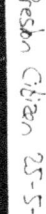

NOTTINGHAM PIRATES 24
PRESTON BOBCATS 14

LOCAL baseball team Preston Bobcats were not able to build upon the previous weekend's league victory as they slumped to defeat after a spirited performance away at Nottingham on Sunday.

The Bobcats started well, keeping the score down to 2-2 after two innings and opened up a 6-4 lead by the end of the third, only to have the home side fight back to make it all square at 10-10 at the end of the fifth.

Conditions, however, conspired against the Bobcats and the problems that they'd had all afternoon coming to terms with an exaggeratedly sloped playing surface came to a head as Nottingham took full advantage to storm into a 20-10 lead in the sixth innings.

Diving

Preston responded well to claw four runs back, only to find themselves behind again to a match-winning 24-14 deficit at the end of the seventh.

For Preston, Laurent Lot and Simon Thynne lead the attack with three runs each and Mark Nickson was outstanding in the unfamiliar position of the centre-field where he made four top class catches - including one spectacular diving effort.

Towards the end, Diana Howarth made Northern Conference history as she became the first girl to play in a senior fixture.

The Bobcats will be hoping to maintain their unbeaten home record this Sunday when they entertain the Hull Royals on Moor Park, pitch off 2pm.

What The Papers Said.......

Presh. Citizen 15-6-95

A SECOND consecutive weekend without a game has left the Preston Bobcats stuck at the foot of BBF Division One North.

The local team will be looking to get back to winning ways — and off the bottom of the division — at Moor Park on Sunday when they entertain fellow strugglers Tamworth Strykers.

The Bobcats have been boosted by the signing of 33-year-old David Farrar from Premier Division side Hounslow Rangers.

Bobcats lose by a whisker

PRESTON BOBCATS 11
HULL ROYALS 12

THE Preston Bobcats lost out by a single, last gasp run in a thrilling encounter at home to the high-flying Hull Royals at Moor Park on Sunday.

The local team had managed to open up a 6-2 lead by the end of the 3rd inning and, in fact, succeeded in keeping Hull scoreless for 6 of the 9 innings.

The visitors pulled 2 runs back for 6-4 in the 5th but runs from Anthony Howarth and Damian Mullen in the 8th looked to have put Preston into an unassailable 8-4 lead.

Hull came out all fired up for the last time, needing to hit 5 runs to pull in front. In fact they hit 7, and leaving the Bobcats having to score 3 to tie the game or 4 to win.

A stirring fightback with runs by Simon Thynne, Pete Howarth and Anthony Howarth saw the score level at 11-11 at the end of the 9th innings - requiring an extra innings to be played to decide the game, during which Hull managed to score, with Preston unable to reply.

A faultless, all round

team performance was typified by Pete Howarth and Anthony Howarth.

Preston team and scorers A Howarth (3), P Howarth (2), Thynne (2), Atack, Hobin, Clugston, Mullen (all), Agnew, Nickson. Breeze.

BASEBALL

Citizen 15 7-95

Bobcats lose out to rivals

BARNSLEY STRIKERS 25
PRESTON BOBCATS 14

PRESTON Bobcats baseball team slumped to their third consecutive away defeat of the season away at mid-table rivals Barnsley on Sunday, despite having stormed into a 12-2 lead after three innings.

A timely change of pitcher by the home side made all the difference and the local side only managed two further runs in the rest of the game. Barnsley struck back with 23 runs the last four innings – including 9 the eighth to take the victory.

Preston switched pitching duties between Alan Milhench, Pete Shone and Damien Mullen but were unable to stem the flow and unluckily, catcher Don McNulty was injured midway through and outfielder David Farrar stepped in to deputise.

Top scorers for the Bobcats were Atack and Mullen with three runs each.

Weekend

Pete Shone also starred with 2 two-base hits which, on an official pitch, would have been home runs.

BBF Division One action returns to Moor Park this Sunday when the Bobcats entertain the Nottingham Pirates, who managed to concede 39 runs at home to Barnsley last weekend. ●

BBC Radio 5 Live were due to be at the Bobcats' midweek training session to record a report for their Straight Up programme, to be broadcast on Saturday at 7.30 pm.

89

What The Papers Said.......

LEP 20-7-95

Call-up for Bobcat pair

★ BIG-hitting Bobcats Damien Mullen and Anthony Howarth have been called into the England baseball squad to face the old enemy from North of the Border. Damien, 27, Cloverfield, Clayton-le-Woods, and Anthony, 19, Downey Road, Ribbleton, Preston, who both play for the Moor Park based Preston Bobcats, are in the 16-man England squad to face the Scots at Perthshire this Sunday.

Picture JOHN HUGHES

Bobcat's deadly duo

TWO Preston Bobcats players figured prominently as the England national baseball team gained a thrilling victory over Scotland in Perth on Sunday.

Newly capped Damien Mullen played for the whole nine innings, scoring three runs and making a superb throw from the outfield to the home plate to get a runner out at a crucial stage of the game.

Anthony Howarth, the youngest member of the squad, was brought on as pitcher in the sixth innings as the team were trailing 8-7, but went on to turn the game around for an England victory of 16-13. Citzen 27 7 95

90

What The Papers Said.......

Bobcats' sudden death clincher

STRETFORD A 15 PRESTON BOBCATS 16

BATTLING Bobcats baseball team withstood a fierce comeback by local rivals Stretford to come away with a last-gasp victory in a stunning match on Sunday.

Preston came out firing on all cylinders and managed to storm to an 11-4 lead by the end of the seventh innings — courtesy of demon pitcher Pete Shone, who pitched a creditable 16 strike outs overall.

Three more runs in the eighth innings would have secured only the Bobcats' second away win of the season.

Incredible

But a close decision went the way of the hosts who then rallied to hit an incredible seven runs to tie the game. A nervy scoreless ninth innings followed, forcing the match into a sudden death extra session, during which the Bobcats outslugged Stretford 5-4 to record an important victory.

Top run scorers for Preston was David Farrar (4) and Pete Howarth (3).

Bobcats now move above Stretford in the league table and look set to finish in a comfortable mid-table position in this, their first season at the higher level.

● Bottom-placed Tamworth Strykers provide the opposition for the Bobcats' next league game at Moor Park on Sunday, pitch off 2pm.

Final flurry for Bobcats

Baseball update

PRESTON Bobcats finished their league season with a win and a defeat in a keenly contested double-header encounter with Tamworth Strykers at Moor Park on Sunday.

In the first game Preston led from the start, scoring 4 runs in the first inning through Howarth, McNulty, Mullen and Shone and a tight defence – led by pitcher Shone with 4 strike-outs – kept the visitors scoreless for 2 of the 5 innings and down to one run in each of the other 3.

Dangerous

Tamworth had looked dangerous at times, but they were unable to produce the runs required and Preston made certain of the win with 4 more runs in the last innings.

In the second game Preston took a 5-1 first innings lead, with Pete Shone and Paul Breeze acting as chief playmakers, each batting in 2 runners.

England international outfielder Damien Mullen had suffered his first strike-outs of the season in the first game and in the second game he was hit twice by the ball as he stood at bat, although he made up for this misfortune by ending up as top scorer with 4 runs (5 in total from the two games).

In the 3rd innings the Bobcats failed to score and the Strykers hit 5 to take the lead.

Using four different pitchers and with wholesale changes in the outfield, Bobcats were still unable to prevent the Strykers hitting another 5 to give a total of 15.

Bobcats needed to hit at least 4 in the 5th to force the visitors to bat again but only managed 2, handing Tamworth a 15-13 victory.

PANTHERS ended the baseball season in fine style by winning the summer tournament played at Moor Park.

As expected, the final showdown against Cartmel proved to be a very tight game – finally taken apart by Chris Addison's grand slam home run which deservedly won him the most valuable player award and a 5-3 win for Panthers.

League president Peter Dyer presented the trophy to team captain for the day, catcher Mark Beattie.

North West Little League Baseball, final positions for 1995: Trafford Saints (won 9 - lost 1); Bolton Knights (8 - 2); Cartmel Valley Lions (5 - 5); Preston Panthers (4 - 6); Kirkby Braves (3 - 7); Holy Family Crosby (1 - 9).

Junior Team News

Preston Panthers is an under 16 team affiliated to the senior Bobcats and the the BBF, Little League and PONY baseball.

The team is coached by Peter Howarth, Frank Caunce and Alan Milhench with valuable support from parents and finished in fourth place in the NW League in 1995. The standings were as follows:

Trafford Saints	9	1
Bolton Knights	8	2
Cartmel Valley Lions	5	5
Preston Panthers	4	6
Kirkby Braves	3	7
Holy Family, Crosby	1	9

Alex McDonald and Christopher Addison were chosen to play for the North West All Star Team who finished runners up to Alconbury US base in the National Championships in July.

Panthers won the North West Summer Tournament at Moor Park on 2nd September with wins of 13-0 over Kirkby and 5-3 in a thrilling final over Cartmel. Chris Addison's grand slam home run doing the damage with Alex pitching for both wins.

Well done and thanks to all who took part this season and to parents for supporting the efforts of the children. We must not forget the community bus driver, Alan Eastwood, for taking us around the county and for taking some good photos and generally showing a keen interest in our activities.

Panthers Team: Christopher Addison, Justin Baron, Gavin Bates, Mark Beattie, Mick Davison, Martin Harris, Claire Hobin, Laura Howarth, Ian Milhench, Matthew Milhench, Alex McDonald, Simon Roberts, Lee Threlfall, David Wearden.

Baseball

☆ **PRESTON BOBCATS** ☆

B·B·F NORTHERN CONFERENCE DIVISION ONE

NEW PLAYERS · OFFICIALS & SUPPORTERS ALWAYS WELCOME

Back cover of the original 1995 edition of "Bobcats Review

A baseball game on our make-shift pitch at Budisov, Czech Republic, Summer 1996

Summer Camps 1996 and 1997

During the long summer breaks from University, I managed to get involved with a volunteer organisation based in Rostock in the north of Germany called Nordeutschejugend In Gemeinschaft (NIG) which organised work camps for people to go off and do interesting things.

In 1996, I was selected to go and accompany groups of children from Rostock, Güstrow and the surrounding area who were going to summer camps being held in the Czech mountains for two weeks at a time.   It wasn't just me – obviously – as, being so shy, I was scared to death for the first week that anybody would talk to me or ask me to do anything. There were 4 or 5 of us and some of the staff changed over with each group while others stayed the whole time.

Aside from just maintaining a general presence and helping out with the various activities, my main contribution was supposed to be teaching everybody how to play baseball.

I had taken a couple of gloves and a couple of bats and a load of tennis balls with me. The bats had to be tied to my rucksack to be transported and stuck out quite menacingly – which caused quite a lot of fuss on the packed train ride from Hamburg.

However, it all went down rather well with everybody on the camp as they had all been brought up in the former GDR and the idea of anything new, commercialised and American was particularly appealing to them at the time.

For me studying German and being interested in their history and the fall of the wall and having been to East Berlin myself in 1990, I found it fascinating to be with these people and to talk about what they remembered about the communist times.

From what I was told, the DDR period was actually pretty good if you fitted in with things. For the kids there were lots of youth groups and organised activities and it was lots of fun.

Obviously, with those regimes having been removed several years before, you have to realise that I was now with a group of people who obviously enjoyed the social and outward bound side of things as they were still doing it even when they didn't "have to" any more – so they might have been a bit biased!

Some of the games they played were certainly throwbacks to that era. There was a card game called "Stasi" where everybody sat round in a circle and had to guess who the Stasi infiltrators in the group were. That sounds a bit sinister nowadays but it was always played in very good humour and was a good way of keeping a group of kids occupied for an hour or so.

So, fairly early on, we organised a big game of baseball with all of the kids and all of the staff taking part. This meant everybody had a go at batting and fielding and got to know a little about how the game was played.

Later on we'd play informally in smaller groups depending on what else was happening and who fancied a game. It was never strictly regimented as the whole thing was meant to be fun – as much for me as for everybody else, as I wasn't getting paid.

PB with baseball group on the sports pitch at Budišov nad Budišovkou, Czech Republic, Summer 1996

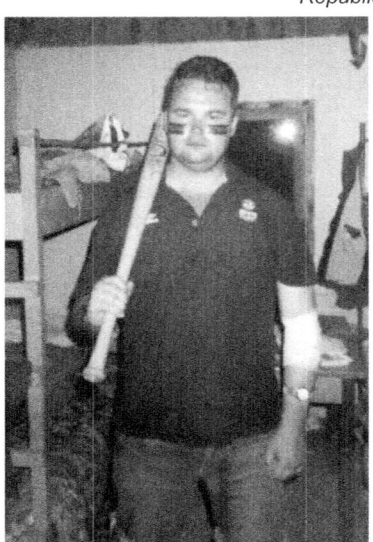

Above: PB umpiring at the Germans v Czechs kids' baseball game, Budišov nad Budišovkou, Czech Republic, Summer 1996.

Left: PB ready for action wearing the away colours "warpaint" of Hansa Rostock in the Germans v Czechs game, Summer 1996

This idea of holiday camps for the kids was very much a Soviet Era sort of thing and there were other groups from Poland and the Czech Republic there at the same time that we were.

It turned out that one of the girls who was looking after the Czech group – Veronika Slehova - was actually a softball coach back home in Ostrava so we arranged to play a proper match at the end of the fortnight – Czechs v Germans - with Veronika and I sharing the bowling and the umpiring when the opposing team was in bat.

The sports field was in a sort of dip with banking on two sides so everybody who came to watch could get a really good view. It was a great atmosphere all round – huge fun to be involved with - and I haven't the faintest clue who won....!

Veronika's boyfriend – a guy called Standa - was a javelin thrower of some repute and he actually trained at the same club as and knew fellow Czech Jan Železný - who was, at that time, the reigning World and Olympic champion and still holds the world record!

What an idyllic setting for playing baseball!
Kunčice pod Ondřejníkem in the Czech Republic, Summer 1997

UCLAN Student Baseball Team, May 1997 (photo by Jill Peacock)

Preston University Team – 1996/97

Once I started at University, I had to work on Sundays – initially at Asda on the security team and later on Kit Kat Radio in Blackpool as well, there was no longer any time free for me to play baseball matches with the Bobcats.

However, Wednesday afternoons are left free at University so that people can play sports - and that's when they arrange all their inter-varsity matches and league competitions.

Having had some involvement with the French Club in my first year (nothing rude – just French language students organising cultural and social events...) I had gained some experience with the setting up of an official Student Union Society.

There was no baseball club there at the time and they were always keen to promote new sports and interests so my application to set up a student baseball club was readily accepted.

One of the conditions of setting up an SU club or society – in order to receive funding for facilities and equipment was that it had to be run properly, prepare accounts and have a managing committee.

Having seen the complications caused by having warring personalities on the French Club committee, I decided to keep this very much "in house", so the committee members for the UCLAN Baseball Club were: me as Chairman, my girlfriend Hanja as Secretary, my brother Gary as Treasurer and his friend James Musgrave.

We all travelled to training sessions together in my car so we had our committee meetings on the way – or occasionally on the way back along with a nice refreshing drink at one of the Docklands pubs.

I'd had some success teaching a basic form of baseball to youth groups of summer camps in the Czech Republic during the summer of 1996 and was fairly sure that I could manage the same with Preston students.

I registered as a coach with the BBF – which, hard to believe, in those days you didn't need any credentials or documentation – you just sent off a cheque for £15 and got a letter back saying that you were registered as a coach for the year...

To be honest, I missed a trick here as I could actually have got PAID for coaching the team. When I made the arrangements in the SU Sports Office, the administrator (no names, no pack-drill) asked me if we needed to bring in a coach for our training sessions as there were funds available to pay for that.

And I rather stupidly said that we didn't need anybody, as I would be able to handle the coaching... Which, I later found out was the

WRONG ANSWER!

It didn't bother me as I had never thought of it as a money generating exercise. We got funds out of the SU sports budget for some equipment – enough fielding gloves for everybody, batting helmets and so on - so I was happy enough with that.

We trained for nothing on the grass at the idyllic Avenham Park in Preston so there was no cost involved for the hire of facilities and apart from any gear that they wanted to buy themselves later, there was no cost to any of our players – which I thought was important for a game that nobody knew if they were going to like or not.

I only found out about the coaching "lark" (to quote an HE Bates Pop Larkin term) during a chance conversation in one of my journalism lectures.

One of my fellow students on the course was a tall Indian guy (I'm really sorry, I can't remember his name) and he had featured in End of the World type (that's a newspaper term for a big dramatic headline) on the back page of the PLUTO student newspaper for getting suspended from his role as coach to the UCLAN basketball team after pushing a referee official during a match.

I commiserated with his fortunes and asked what was likely to come of the pending investigation. He said that he had appealed and expected to be "working again" soon.

That always seemed to me to be an odd choice of words until it eventually dawned on me that, as the head coach of an SU team – particularly a competitive SU team in the Uni leagues – then he would probably be getting paid out of the SU Sports Coaching budget for his time. That's when I realised that I had dropped a bit of a clanger and could probably have done the same... Oh well....

Anyway, we set up a stall at Freshers' Fair 1996 in order to attract some members to join our fledgling club. I made some exhibits up with some photos of me playing with the Bobcats and playing with the kids at the summer camp and to my pleasant surprise, we signed up 7 or 8 prospective players.

I won't go through who they were now – although I do remember most of them, if not all by name. There was a guy and his girlfriend who wanted to sign up for an sports activity that they could take part in together (bear in mind that most of the other properly organised sports had separate men's and women's teams whereas we took just about anybody...) – several more girls and a couple of boys who, dare I say it were not particularly sporty – but who cares, it was meant to be fun.

We put up posters around the Students Union as well and attracted a girl from Holland – where they do / did actually play softball in schools, I believe, plus an English guy who had been living in Holland as well. Gary brought a few people in as well from his course so we had a decent little gathering for our first training session on the park.

I was rather surprised that we never actually found any "proper" experienced baseball players. By that I mean anybody else other than me who had ever played for a team before anywhere else.

In view of the fact that there were a lot of teams in the North West – in Preston, Liverpool, Manchester and across Yorkshire – many of them having junior teams as well, I find this a bit odd . But at least it meant that we didn't have any clash of personalities with people coming in and thinking that they knew more than me, so I didn't really mind.

After all, it's actually a lot easier to teach people basic skills completely from scratch because they won't have picked up any bad habits that they need to unlearn.

So we had a few sessions on the park during October and early November until the weather became too bad to make it worth arranging for outdoors any more.

We warmed up with a few throwing exercises – like I had learnt with the Bobcats - then we practiced batting and fielding and finished off with a bit of game between however many people were there on any given day. And that gave everybody a chance to practice running between the bases and the fielders trying to get them out.

One thing that we never actually did properly was pitching - ie bowling the ball in the correct baseball manner – mainly because I had never leant how to do it.

Pitching is very specialised and I didn't want to try and teach it and get it wrong as that might demoralise an otherwise keen group of players – and maybe give them an incorrect technique

I thought it more important to keep it fun for everybody and get them all playing at a basic level, so decided not to worry about insisting on a skill that they might never have to use.

Three photos of training with the University team at Avenham Park in Preston (1997)

Instead, we just bowled underarm for our training sessions as that was easy enough to do and it meant that most people could have a go at bowling as well as batting and fielding.

James Musgrave managed to find us a cost free venue that we could use on Wednesday afternoons during the winter months so that we could keep the team together and still do some training activities during the bad weather.

He somehow arranged for us to use the sports hall at Tulketh High School in Preston for two hours on the agreement, that once the weather was better later in the year we would do some coaching with the school children out on the playing field.

The gym hall had basketball hoops mounted at either end and there was a stash of various sports equipment in a recess in one corner so we started off our indoor sessions by playing a bit of basketball to loosen up.

I read somewhere once that basketball was actually originally invented by a baseball coach who wanted an indoor activity to keep his player fit and sharp during the winter months so, in that case, we were continuing a long tradition!

But, unlike the famous basketball inventing baseball coach of old, and thanks to modern production techniques, artificial materials and the consumer society, we were able to get hold of some light foam spongey balls – about the size of tennis balls - to use.

These were just heavy enough so that you could pitch them properly and hit them far enough to make it a worthwhile training exercise, but at the same time, light enough so that they didn't cause any damage if they hit against the windows, light fittings or squashy body parts and this meant that we were able to practice batting, throwing and fielding as well.

It turned out that the weather was very bad over the winter and it always seemed to rain on a Wednesday afternoon so we were very lucky that we were able to hold our training sessions in the gym.

In that respect, we were a lot better off than many of the other – more established - sports clubs who had their outdoor training sessions and matches washed out.

In the end I seem to remember there was some sort of problem with the grass on the school field. I don't recall the details - I think it had been so mulched up by the bad weather that they decided to re-seed it or something...

Anyway, it was never possible for us to do any coaching with the pupils out of the field, which was a bit of a shame and, as soon as the weather improved, we were back out in the fresh air in Avenham Park again.

Now, it is very difficult to arrange anything much for the end of the University year, as after the Easter Holidays, people tend to start having exams and coursework to hand in - and the foreign students start disappearing.

Certainly any students in their final year would have a very stressful workload with final exams approaching and dissertations to finish, so we fully acknowledged that numbers would start dropping off from May onwards – which was unfortunate as that was when the official club baseball season was just getting under way.

In order to give the players a treat and allow the players to experience the thrill of a proper game before they went their separate ways for the summer, I contacted Frank Caunce and arranged a Sunday afternoon match against the Preston Bobcats at their Moor Park venue.

Sadly, because I had to work on Sundays, I was unable to take part in the actual game so the players were thrown in at the deep end a bit but Frank took them in hand and made sure they all did the right things.

I stopped off at the park on my way between jobs and was able to see how things were going and take a few photos.

Acknowledging that there was a huge gap in playing standards, Frank had mixed the teams up a bit so that some of the Bobcats players could play alongside the students and help them with what they should be doing.

Everybody seemed to enjoy themselves and it was a good early season run out for the Bobcats team before they got to play the majority of their league fixtures.

For our student players, we achieved what I had hoped for and they got the opportunity to play in a real baseball match, and I don't think anybody minded that our team were easily beaten...

In the evening after the game, I rang Pauline Howarth - who did all the score-sheets for the Bobcats games - and I got the match details from her. She gave me the innings scores and run of play and any interesting playing statistics for the student players and I was able to write a match report for the PLUTO newspaper.

I submitted it on the Sunday night, along with the team photo that we had taken at Avenham Park the week before, and was very pleased to think that I was going to be able to get some recognition for the players who had put so much work into learning a new sport over the course of the year.

But – would you believe it – the PLUTO editor (who I'd had several run ins with in the past) came back to me and said that it was too late to go in the final edition of the year as their deadline had been on Friday.

I argued that this was rather short-sighted in view of the fact that a lot of people did sports over the weekend – plus how much work were they likely to have done on the student newspaper between Friday and Monday, anyway...? But it was to no avail – they wouldn't budge on the deadline issue.

So, in a fit of pique, I quickly produced a mock up of the back page of the student newspaper on my computer at home. I called it "Plus Tôt" as a play on words with the actual real life title and also a vague sarcastic – and obscure - joke in French about the "early" deadline.

I inserted the team photo of the student baseball players as the main picture and filled the rest of the page with my match report. I then got a large amount of copies printed off and put them up on every notice board around the University that I could find, ironically scooping the official PLUTO publication date of the Friday by 4 days...

Unfortunately, I had my year abroad the following year so I wasn't able to go back to Preston and restart the SU Baseball team and, without me being there, nothing else happened with it.

By the time I got back to the university in September 1998, the other members of the original committee were no longer there and many of the original players had either finished their studies while I was away, or had moved on, or dropped out -   or were now too busy concentrating on other things.

I didn't really have the enthusiasm - bearing in mind that this was going to be my all-important final degree year - to strike out on my own and try and start it all again from scratch, so that was – sadly – the end of my association with baseball. For the time being...

PB's brother Gary and James Musgrave at the game against Preston Bobcats

James Musgrave batting for the UCLAN Pirates against the Preston Bobcats. Frank Caunce is the Umpire standing behind the catcher (Photo by Paul Breeze)

Left: Technically in Czechoslovakia, September 1990 (Photo by Graham Hill)

Middle Photos: Really in Czechoslovakia.
Left: PB in Wenceslas Square, Prague. Right: Inter-Railing companion Simon Blanchard with PB's Czech penfriend Aleš at Karlstejn Castle – both September 1991.

Bottom Photos:
Left: Summer Camp at Budisov,CZ, 1996

Right: Michael Spickermann, Petra Krull & Thilo Fangk outside a mountain top restaurant near Kunčice, CZ 1997.

Youth group at Kunčice pod Ondřejníkem in the Czech Republic, Summer 1997

The Day I Invented A Cricket / Baseball Hybrid Game

As a young child, I was always fascinated by Czechoslovakia. Not the people, or the culture, or the country's history – after all, how is a 7 or 8 year old growing up in Peterborough in the 1970s going to know much about that.... – but the actual word itself.

In my class room at school we had a Ladybird book of flags – or whatever it was – and I liked looking through it and seeing all the different designs and colours.

I was especially drawn to any flag that was red white and blue – like ours – but found the French and Dutch flags a bit boring as they only had straight lines of colour. The Luxembourg flag also didn't count as it had the wrong colour blue – but the Czechoslovakian flag had the right colours and a more interesting design because of the triangle shape on the left hand side.

What I liked most about Czechoslovakia was that it was the longest named country in the flag book and I knew how to spell it.

Now, I was a bit of a clever clogs back in Primary School – I once wrote all my answers to a times table test in roman numerals to demonstrate that I knew them all. The teacher – who I won't name – appeared not to appreciate my cleverness here and I got given a 0 for my mark, even though I actually gave all the right answers, which I thought was a little unfair.

Funnily enough, in our modern enlightened times, my actions would probably have given rise to a class discussion about different cultures and numbering systems and possibly "what the Romans did for us" but back then I was just "wrong" for some reason...

So, anyway, I used to use the word "Czechoslovakia" as often as possible whenever I was writing something at school to show off that I knew how to spell it, even if I actually knew nothing about the place.

I remember attempting to shoehorn "supercalifragilisticexpiali-docious" (that's the song from the Mary Poppins film) into a story once but couldn't work out how to spell it – and, needless to say, as a 7 year old, I'd never heard of "antidisestablish-mentarianism", otherwise I'd probably have found lots of uses for that one as well.

While we are on this subject – and getting things off our chest that have wrankled for years and years (bear grudges – moi? surely not...):

Once, in infants' school, I was writing a story about kids playing cowboys and Indians and I was using reported speech (which may, admittedly, have been a bit advanced for my Janet and John age group at the time – but, heigh ho...) and I quoted the Indian-playing kid as saying something like:

"me go home for tea now – time to stop ze game"

and the bloody teacher woman - rather than realising that I was being amazingly clever and quoting how he would have sounded in his put-on "Red Indian" accent – suggested that I had written it badly and criticised my spelling! But there you go...

To the best of my knowledge, I never met a Czechoslovakian person until I visited my penfriend in Prague in 1991. There may well have been Czechs living in Peterborough when I was growing up as there were a lot of Central and Eastern Europeans who had been displaced by the Second World War and the various upheavals afterwards and there is NOW quite a large Czech community and Honorary Consulate in the City but that's all quite recent, I believe.

When I was little, the largest ex-pat community in our area was Italian as lots of Italians had come over after the war to work in the brickyards which were all around Fletton, Stanground, Yaxley and Whittlesey.

We had Italian families living next door to us for a number of years - who we got on very well with - and my comprehensive school offered Italian as a foreign language as there was a desire within the Italian community for their children to learn "proper Italian" rather than just knowing the various regional dialects that they spoke at home.

There were also a lot of Polish people in our area and we had the Polish Ex Servicemens' Club in what used to be Stanground Vicarage down by the church.

I believe that there was a sizeable Ukrainian community elsewhere in the city – at least there used to be a Ukrainian social club in the town centre - and there was also a large Caribbean and Asian presence as well.

On my first ever day at Southfields infants' school, I sat next to Suzanna Mankiewski (that may not be how her name was spelt – I apologise if it's wrong...) and throughout my school years, I was always in the same classes as Diana Pacocha, who had Polish parents but was herself born in Peterborough - so I have always been used to being surrounded by people of other nationalities and being exposed to the use of other languages.

I have been lucky enough to visit Czechoslovakia / the Czech Republic on three separate occasions - Prague in 1991 (back when it was still part of Czechoslovakia) and summer camps in the Moravian mountains near Olomouc in 1996 and 1997.

I was also "technically" in Czechoslovakia in September 1990 when on a holiday in Poland, albeit for a very brief period, when I straddled the border markers up on a snow covered mountain top and stood in both countries at once for a few seconds...

I have written a bit about the Summer Camps already and will cover my other travels in more detail on another occasion so that you don't lose interest as this is supposed to be a book about cricket and baseball, after all - and you want to hear all about the day that I invented a cricket / baseball hybrid game!

I was volunteering as a Youth Leader with a group of children from the former East German towns of Rostock and Gustrow and we were in a residential youth camp in the middle of nowhere in the picturesque Czech mountains.

I might point out here, for anybody who thinks that the Czech Republic is essentially just "Prague" – rather like most foreigners who think that Britain and London are the same thing and don't realise that we have countryside as well.... that, despite being a relatively small country (and one that I really love) I have to say that a surprisingly large proportion of the Czech Republic is in the middle of nowhere and is incredibly wild!

In fact, when I was on the train between Dresden and Prague in 1991, the route snaked its way through the most beautiful mountainous landscape - but an observant co-traveller pointed out that you could see why the Nazis opted to annex the Sudetenland rather than trying to invade across that difficult terrain!

But, back to the summer of 1997. After a few days of heavy rain, the grassy playing areas where we would normally be playing games had turned into a swamp and we were running out of things to do to keep the kids occupied.

There were about 40 of them aged, I seem to think, 12 to 18, so there was a lot of energy that needed burning up and a lot of time to kill 24 hours a day for the two week visit – and there's only so much that you can do with a table tennis table in the hall before people start getting bored...

We'd had a couple of "Schlammschlacht" (mud fights) which were fun in the moment but necessitated a lot of cleaning up afterwards and, one afternoon, we really hit rock bottom when the only new and original thing that anybody could think of to do was to smear make-up on our faces and prance around the campsite dressed up as women to entertain the children.

Needless to say, this wasn't my idea but I went along with it - purely in the spirit of helping to keep everybody occupied for an hour or so - and let one of the girls give me some sort of awful makeover. I then tied the tails of my shirt up in a bow across my midriff - to affect girly attire - and stuffed the front with socks to create some semblance of cleavage - and that was my contribution.

Once we had been paraded around all the kids' cabins and the joke had worn off, we all trooped up to the Penzion Krkoška further up the hill - which was run by the guy who owned the campsite - for a few Czech beers and to give the locals a laugh...

So, set against this dubious backdrop of events, you can see why everybody was overjoyed when – with it still chucking it down the next day - I volunteered to devise an energetic activity that would keep everybody occupied all afternoon.

I had my baseball gear with me so took out the bat and then found a sturdy cardboard box about 3 feet high round the back of the kitchen.

I folded the table tennis table up and pushed it to one side of the hall and then looked around trying to work out what sort of game we could have.

Even today – 25 years later - I can still remember the anxious feeling that I had, pacing up and down in the hall swinging my bat by my side, head down in an attempt to avoid to the excited expectant looks of the gathering masses who were waiting to be entertained - and me wondering what the hell to do next!

All eyes were upon me so in my rather basic German, I put on a huge act of confidence and set out to explain the rules of a game that didn't quite exist.

And it went something like this: I stood the box against the back wall. That was to be the wicket. The batter would stand in front of it holding the baseball bat and had to defend the wicket from the bowled ball. Luckily, we had some soft spongy tennis balls to use which wouldn't do any damage indoors and also wouldn't hurt if you got hit by them.

Knowing that everybody likes batting and that everybody (except Graham Hill...) hates fielding, I placed myself as bowler so that I could also act as umpire. I then selected a couple of the older boys to act as fielders /catchers and the rest of group waited for their turn to bat.

I bowled the ball at the wicket and the batter tried to hit the ball. If I hit the wicket, they were out and had to join the fielders. If they hit the ball, they had to drop the bat and run to the other end of the hall where, by touching the end wall, they were "safe".

If the ball was caught before it bounced off the floor or walls, then they were out and had to join the fielders - and they were also out if the fielders retrieved the ball and tagged them with it while they were running to the far end.

Once the next batter hit the ball, the waiting batter(s) at the safe end could run back to the batting end. If they got back to the batting wall without getting tagged with the ball, they were safe and could rejoin the queue to bat again. If they got tagged out, they joined the fielders.

As you can see, this was basically an indoor version of Danish Longball - which we used to play in class groups at primary school – with the addition of cricket stumps and a bit of British Bulldog or tiggy thrown in as well.

At break times at primary school, we always used to play "Tiggy with Wiggy" which, unlike cricket, you CAN actually play with just 2 or 3 people.

One person is "on" or "it" they have to tig somebody else and then they are on. (I believe this is what is referred to as the game of "He" in Enid Blyton's books). In this game there is usually a "homey" area where you are safe from being tigged and, in our Tiggy with Wiggy games, this used to be the semi-circles at either end of the netball court on the big playground.

So you can see how I came up with the rules of this hybrid one-off indoor game.

"Wiggy", by the way, was the nickname for one of our friends from school. I believe it originally came from the character in the Bash Street Dogs comic strip in The Beano. He is a top solicitor in London these days so I won't mention his name in print, just in case....

To the full credit of the kids who were playing my game, they all fully entered into the spirit and, after a while, they started to get quite tactical. The batters realised that if they waited until there was a large enough group of them waiting on the safe wall, then they had a much better chance of getting back to base if they all ran at once.

The fielders, at the same time, (and without me having to suggest it - which was positive as it showed that they were giving the game some thought...) quickly developed the skill of retrieving the ball, tagging one runner with it and throwing it to another fielder to tag another runner as part of the same play.

Obviously, as the game progressed, there were gradually more fielders and fewer runners so the tactics became more important.

There weren't any scores involved in this game – that would have been much too complicated – and we just carried on until everybody was out.

The good thing is that everybody seemed to enjoy themselves – even me, once I had settled on what we were doing – and we carried on playing until teatime, by which time everybody was completely knackered!

Luckily, the next day brought better weather and everywhere began drying out so we were able to resume our usual outdoor activities.

But that, in a nutshell, is the story of how I once came to invent a cricket / baseball hybrid game in the Czech Republic!

Top photo: Bored puppy syndrome –
let's play at dressing up...!
Kunčice,1997.

Bottom photos: My favourite Czechs!

Left - PB with Iva Ledvonova who
worked in the kitchen at the Kunčice
camp we visited in 1997 (photo by
Suzana Oblukova)

Above Right: Suzana Oblukova – Suzi
- who helped out as local interpreter for
us at both Czech camps I went to in
1996 and 1997 (Photo by Paul Breeze)

Keep in touch with what's happening
in British Baseball, call the
British Baseball Federation Hotline.

BBF HOTLINE

0891 884533

Calls charged at 36p per minute off-peak,
48p per minute peak time.

BBF Hotline Manager - 1997

I was also employed for a short while as the Telephone Hotline Manager for the British Baseball Federation. Back in the days before everything was easily accessible on the internet, this was a premium rate telephone service where you could ring up and find out all the weekends results. There was a similar "Heineken Hotline" for ice hockey results as well – and for all sorts of other sports, I imagine, as well...

Basically on a Sunday evening, I would get a fax with all the results from the various leagues across the country and would dial up the hotline access number. I then had to input a code and was able to record a long message with all the information of the week.

I was supposed to get paid a % of the takings from the premium rate line but don't actually remember ever getting any money for it. But it was interesting to do and it does give me an unusual entry on my media CV.

A particularly sad duty I had to perform media-wise was in the summer of 1997 when Frank collapsed and died of a heart attack on the way to a Sunday afternoon away game. In true Frank fashion, those who were with him at time said that he was more concerned about getting the kit to the sports field so that the junior team would be able to play than about his own health situation.

On that evening's BBF Hotline recording, I gave a notice about Frank's sad death before launching into the other business of the day. We also got a nice piece about him in the Preston Citizen.*

After Frank's passing, and with my year abroad for University coming in 1997/98, I lost touch with the Bobcats team - and the University team that we had built up in 1996/97 had all gone their separate ways by the time I got back to Preston in September 1998.

It was my final year of my degree and I figured I'd be best served doing a bit of work - so I never got fully back into baseball again.

But, I still have all the gear stashed away somewhere – and my university team shirt still fits – so, as Sean Connery said in that not very good knock-off Bond film, "never say never"...!!

*As well as being a talented artist, Frank was also a very good musician and could play a variety of different instruments. He played trumpet in a local jazz band and the band played at his funeral.

PB on radio duty at a car racing event at Mondercange in Luxembourg in August 1997

Baseball Post Script 1997/98

I spent a year in the Grand Duchy of Luxembourg for my French language year abroad that was a requirement of my university course. If you want to know how I ended up going there – as opposed to Montpellier in the south of France, where most of the other people from my year went, you can read all about it in great detail in North / South Divide Volume 2 - but it's not necessary to go into all again here for the purposes of this particular story.

The only thing you need to know is that it is due to BASEBALL that I came to meet my wife Lucy.

The odd thing was that I never actually played any baseball in Luxembourg, nor even came across anybody else who did.

For my year abroad I had a placement with a media agency who produced a local Saar/Lorr/Lux business magazine (for the Saarland / Lorraine / Luxembourg region), had some involvement as the local agents for Paris Match (but I never actually discovered what...) and also produced a daily round-up of the Luxembourgish press for the European Commission.

That was interesting but involved getting up early as I had to go down to the railway station to pick up the newspapers every morning as soon as they arrived and before they were delivered to the shops.

I also discovered that, in the basement of the same building as the media agency, there was the studio of a commercial radio station called WAKY 107FM which was part of the Programme Europe 2 network and which broadcast certain programmes in English at different times of the day.

This was a sort of local successor to the famous Radio Luxembourg of old and had been set up by Bob Christie who had previously worked on that station.

If you want to know more about commercial radio in Luxembourg, you can refer to my university dissertation *"The BBC And Radio Luxembourg: A Comparison Of Broadcasting Styles and Attitudes"* (ISBN 9781727867022) which, by happy coincidence, is available by mail order from Amazon, Posh Up North, Book Depository and many other quality outlets.

Anyway, enough of the advertising.... I wangled a meeting with Bob and, after hearing about my radio experience back in England, he gave me a job as presenter, initially doing stand-in work to cover for when one of the regulars was unavailable.

I don't know if it is still going, but when I was there, there was an English language magazine in Luxembourg called "Luxembourg News" and it was aimed at the English and American ex-pats who lived in the Grand Duchy. It came out once a week and had news of events, adverts and letters and all sorts of other things to keep people in touch with what was going on.

Being new to the area and hardly knowing anybody, I thought it might be a good way of meeting people to enquire whether there was a group who played baseball or who might like to start one up, so I wrote a letter in to the Lux News and it got printed the following week.

I had a couple of people reply to me – one was an American woman who everybody at the radio station knew and suggested I avoid like the plague, and there was somebody else that I can't remember now – It was a long time ago.

But after that I was taken on permanently on the radio and got involved in other things so nothing more ever came of the baseball idea – or so I thought at the time.....

Completely unknown to me, elsewhere in the Grand Duchy, Lucy had seen my letter in the Lux News and thought that baseball would be a good energetic activity for her teenage sons to get involved with. But she was about to take them on a trip to England for a couple of weeks and she put the magazine aside to look at again when they got back.

Apparently, when she got back from England, she couldn't find the magazine again and so had to give up on the idea.

For anybody who remembers, this was the time when Princess Diana was killed in the car crash in the tunnel in Paris. On that Saturday night in question, I had been helping Bob Christie from Radio WAKY do a disco at a weekend equestrian gala event at the horse riding club in Merl and when I got home - late - I saw on the news that Diana had been injured in an accident and taken to hospital.

The next morning when I woke up, it was reported that she had died at the hospital, so that was quite a memorable occasion for me one way or the other.

Shortly after all this, I was presenting a show on the radio one day and got a phone call in the studio from this Lucy woman.

The station was very keen on receiving listener feedback and was always encouraging people to phone in for competitions or with requests.

It turned out that she was a big fan of the station and she was often able to have it on in the background in her office where she was working as a secretary.

She asked me if I was the same "Paul Breeze" who had put the piece in the Lux News about baseball – because she had wanted to get in touch and then lost the magazine - and I replied that I was but that nothing more had come of it.

PB in the Radio WAKY 107FM studio in Luxembourg in December 1997 (Photo by Isabelle Mosar)

World Champion F1 driver Michael Schumacher at a media event in Luxembourg, September 1997 (Photo by Paul Breeze)

She then said (while I had the telephone receiver wedged between my chin and shoulder and was expertly trying to get the next CD cued up and levelled at the same as talking ...) that she'd had a neighbour called Paul Breeze when she was little, living in Kent and was I related to them?

I replied that, to the best of my knowledge, I wasn't related because my Breeze family all came from the Ramsey area in Cambridgeshire, although my granddad Whittington's family had started off in Kent.

Anyway, after that we talked quite often on the phone when I was working in the studio and Lucy sometimes sent me faxes with requests.

The standing instructions at the station were that you HAD to stick to the playlist because it had been expertly constructed to provide the correct mix of music for the show – but that if you received a request from a listener then you had to make your best efforts to play it.

So then Lucy helped me – at my instigation - to develop a list of bogus listeners from different locations around the Grand Duchy within the broadcast area of the WAKY station so that I could manipulate the playlist with more music that I wanted to play.

I actually met Lucy for the first time when I was presenting my - by then – regular morning show on the radio and she came in to the offices to record some voiceovers for an advert – (Bob Christie regular brought in different people that he knew to do this so as not to have all the same voices all the time. They didn't get paid anything for their services as he expected them to do it purely for the "thrill" of being involved in radio...!)

I did several advert voice-overs while I was there as well. Unpaid – naturally....

It was usually a case of, after I'd my finished my show (which I DID get paid for, albeit not a huge amount ...) "Ooh - while you're here can you just do this for me...?"

I was the voice of Papa Joe's cafe for a year or so – they also did outside catering and I had to do a whole spiel in French about the services they offered. The backing music to the advert was "Poppa Joe" by the Sweet and I still look upon it as a super piece of radio on my part.

I also did one in English for a company who I think were called Balloons Deluxe who offered hot air balloon trips.

And I was also a "Spice Boy" (don't ask...) along with some of the other male presenters promoting some sort of event or other – I don't remember what it was now.....

One of the other presenters who she knew already - and who knew that I had been chatting with her on the phone a lot – brought her in to meet me and that was that. I didn't have much time to talk as I was in the middle of doing my show but it was nice to put a face to a name.

Shortly before Christmas 1997 one of the people at the media company who was involved with a children's cancer charity was organising an appeal for toys for Christmas. I enthusiastically pushed this appeal during my radio shows and Lucy offered to get her sons to donate some things that they had grown out of.

So, one evening, I went over to her house to pick up the donations and met the rest of the family.

The rest of the story has no connection to baseball whatsoever so doesn't really fit in with the scope of this particular book. However, I am sure that I will tell it all at some point or other, in a future volume.

Suffice it to say, that it all turned out well – and is still going well some 24 years later!

Paul and Lucy officiating at an ice hockey tournament in Widnes, July 12018 (photo by Geoff White)

NORTH / SOUTH DIVIDE
WHY NOT COLLECT THE SET?

North / South Divide: The Original

RANDOM RAMBLINGS ABOUT
BRITISH ICE HOCKEY DURING THE
2013/14 SEASON

By Paul Breeze

ISBN: 979-8563183759

The 2013/14 season was a watershed year for me ice hockey wise. The Fylde Flyers team finished, leaving me with only recreational hockey to write about in Blackpool so I decided to branch out and cover the English National League in a more general manner.

I was kindly taken on by Blueliner.com as a guest writer where I was able to submit opinionated rants and occasional news stories as it suited me and I also started doing weekend round ups of all the league games on my own general Best Kept Secrets news and reviews website as well.

As I was being encouraged to widen the scope of the season review book that I had started to produce (and hopefully sell…), it made sense to set up my own dedicated ice hockey news website and this is how the Ice Hockey Review grass roots ice hockey website was born.

What you will find in this book is a mixture of opinion columns written for Blueliner.com and round-ups and news items that started off on bestkeptsecrets and, after January 2014, ended up on icehockeyreview.co.uk. I hope that makes sense – it shouldn't be boring, anyway…!

Volume 2: Ice Hockey And Me

I put this book together as a sort of a "self-healing project" after a bout of ill health during 2020 that made me realise that, if anything happened to me, there's a whole raft of interesting anecdotes, memories and funny stories that might otherwise be lost to the world - and I thought I ought to write them all down for the benefit of future generations.

So, if you are interested in ice hockey trivia and have the slightest interest in such bizarre topics as:

How I came to be at the World Championships in Luxembourg,
The day I met Stewart Roberts,
Which Sims twin is which and
The story behind Lucy's "French And Ormes" poem,

then this is definitely the book for you!

ISBN: 9781909643451

Printed in Great Britain
by Amazon